The Resurgence of the Unified Arab Investment Agreement and the Organisation for Islamic Cooperation Investment Agreement

AF714838

International Investment Law and Arbitration

Editors-in-Chief
Ian A. Laird (*Crowell & Moring; Columbia Law School; Georgetown University Law Center; International Law Institute*)
Borzu Sabahi (*Curtis, Mallet-Prevost, Colt & Mosle LLP; Georgetown University Law Center; International Law Institute*)

Managing Editor
Giovanna E. Gismondi (*Managing Director, International Investment Law Center – Georgetown University*)

Editorial Advisory Board
Alvaro Galindo (*Georgetown University*) – Mark Kantor (*Independent arbitrator; Georgetown University*) – Antonio R. Parra (*Independent Consultant*) – Sylvie Tabet (*Trade Law Bureau, Government of Canada*) – Anne Marie Whitesell (*Georgetown University Law Center*)

Editorial Board
David L. Attanasio (*Dechert LLP*) – Crina Baltag (*Stockholm University*) – Brooks W. Daly (*Permanent Court of Arbitration*) – Nicholas J. Diamond (*Georgetown University*) – Kabir Duggal (*Arnold & Porter LLP*) – Erica Franzetti (*Georgetown University*) – Kiran Nasir Gore (*George Washington University Law School*) – Joongi Kim (*Yonsei Law School*) – John Laird (*Crowell & Moring*) – Juan Felipe Merizalde (*Adell & Merizalde*) – Frédéric G. Sourgens (*Washburn University School of Law*) – Prof. Dr. Mohamed Abdel Wahab (*Zulficar & Partners*) – Todd Weiler (*Independent counsel, consultant, expert, and arbitrator*) – Diora M. Ziyaeva (*Dentons LLP*)

Volumes published in this Brill Research Perspectives title are listed at *brill.com/rpi*

The Resurgence of the Unified Arab Investment Agreement and the Organisation for Islamic Cooperation Investment Agreement

A Dawn of a New Chapter on Investment Protection?

By

Mohamed S. Abdel Wahab and Kabir Duggal

BRILL

LEIDEN | BOSTON

This paperback book edition is simultaneously published as issue 4.1–2 of *International Investment Law a*
Arbitration, DOI:10.1163/24055778-12340011.

Typeface for the Latin, Greek, and Cyrillic scripts: "Brill". See and download: brill.com/brill-typeface.

ISBN 978-90-04-53315-8 (paperback)
ISBN 978-90-04-53317-2 (e-book)

Copyright 2022 by Mohamed S. Abdel Wahab and Kabir Duggal. Published by Koninklijke Brill NV, Leiden, The Netherlands.
Koninklijke Brill NV incorporates the imprints Brill, Brill Nijhoff, Brill Hotei, Brill Schöningh, Brill Fink, Brill mentis, Vandenhoeck & Ruprecht, Böhlau and V&R unipress.
Koninklijke Brill NV reserves the right to protect this publication against unauthorized use. Requests for re-use and/or translations must be addressed to Koninklijke Brill NV via brill.com or copyright.com.

This book is printed on acid-free paper and produced in a sustainable manner.

Contents

The Resurgence of the Unified Arab Investment Agreement and the Organisation for Islamic Cooperation Investment Agreement

A Dawn of a New Chapter on Investment Protection?

Professor Dr. Mohamed S. Abdel Wahab
Professor of International Arbitration, Private International Law and English Contract Law, Cairo University
Founding Partner & Head of International Arbitration, Construction and Energy Groups
MSW@zulficarpartners.com

Dr. Kabir Duggal
Lecturer-in-Law, Columbia Law School; SJD Candidate, Harvard Law School
kabir.duggal@columbia.edu

Abstract

Multilateral investment treaties (MITs) are international legal instruments whose purpose is to, *inter alia*, facilitate social and economic cooperation on regional and/or global scales. While there is abundant literature and decisions on MITs generally, there has been scant analysis of such instruments executed in the Arab and Muslim-majority worlds.

This book discusses two such instruments: the Unified Agreement for the Investment of Arab Capital in the Arab States and the Organisation of Islamic Cooperation Agreement for Promotion, Protection and Guarantee of Investments Among Member States. These investment agreements are among the oldest MITs in the modern world. The UAA was approved at the 11th Arab Summit Conference held in Amman, Jordan, in November 1980. The OIC Agreement was opened for signature on June 1–5, 1981 and entered into force on February 25, 1988. It is only recently, however, that these two long-dormant treaties have acquired special significance. This book provides a comprehensive, critical review of these two treaties that remain to be fully tested and utilized.

© MOHAMED S. ABDEL WAHAB AND KABIR DUGGAL, 2022 | DOI:10.1163/9789004533172_002

Keywords

Middle East – North Africa – MENA Region – investment protection – Unified Agreement for the Investment of Arab Capital in the Arab States – Organisation of Islamic Cooperation Agreement for Promotion – Protection and Guarantee of Investments Among Member States

1 Introduction

Multilateral investment treaties (MITs) are international legal instruments whose purpose is to facilitate social and economic cooperation on a global scale. While there is abundant literature and precedent on MITs generally, there has been scant analysis of such instruments executed in the Arab and Muslim-majority worlds.

This book discusses two such instruments: the Unified Agreement for the Investment of Arab Capital in the Arab States (the "Unified Arab Agreement" or "UAA")[1] and the Organisation of Islamic Cooperation ("OIC") Agreement for Promotion, Protection and Guarantee of Investments Among Member States ("OIC Agreement").[2] These investment agreements are among the oldest MITs in the world. The UAA was approved at the 11th Arab Summit Conference held in Amman, Jordan, in November 1980. The OIC Agreement was opened for signature on June 1-5, 1981 and entered into force on February 25, 1988. It is only recently, however, that these two long-dormant treaties have acquired special significance.

Before discussing the treaties' growing role, it is important to distinguish between the overlapping territories covered by these two treaties: the Arab world and the Muslim-majority world. The Arab world consists of 22 Arabic-speaking States, most of which are located in the Middle East and North Africa. While all Arab States are currently Muslim-majority countries, Arabs are a minority in the broader Muslim-majority world.[3]

The term "Muslim-majority world" refers to the vast, diverse region comprising the band of countries with majority Muslim populations that stretches

1 Unified Agreement for the Investment of Arab Capital in the Arab States, Economic Documents, No. 3 (Tunis: League of Arab States) (adopted 27 Nov 1980, entered into force 9 Sept 1981).

2 Agreement for Promotion, Protection and Guarantee of Investments Among Member States of the Organisation of the Islamic Conference (signed 5 June 1981, entered into force 25 February 1988).

3 *Demographics of Islam*, BERKLEY CENTER FOR RELIGION, PEACE & WORLD AFFAIRS, https://berkleycenter.georgetown.edu/essays/demographics-of-islam.

from western Africa to Indonesia. The Muslim-majority world is far from homogenous, as its inhabitants adhere to several interpretations of Islam and a myriad of other religions, speak dozens of languages, display diverse phenotypical features, observe manifold customs and cultural norms, and participate in a wide array of political and economic systems. Because the Muslim-majority world subsumes the Arab world[4] – and because all Arab member-States are also OIC member-States – this book will use the term "Muslim-majority world" to refer to both concepts collectively.

The Muslim-majority world is home to many of the most challenging and complex issues in global politics. For example, the Israeli-Palestinian conflict has long been a subject of international attention. More recently, a series of uprisings and revolutions in the early 2010s – known as the "Arab Spring" – threatened to usher in a new political order in much of the Arab world. Many of the high-profile military engagements of the 21st century have been fought in Muslim-majority States, particularly in Syria, Iraq, Afghanistan, Yemen, and Libya. Global powers such as the United States, Russia, and the United Kingdom have directly participated in these hostilities.

The Muslim-majority world is also of great significance to the international economy. As the bridge between Europe, Africa, and Asia, it lies at the center of global trade. Muslim-majority States are home to approximately 24% of the world's population[5] and generate 24% of the global Gross Domestic Product (GDP).[6] They play an outsized role in global energy production and are responsible for nearly half of the world's petroleum output.[7] Muslim-majority States are also critical stakeholders in the investor-State dispute settlement system: nearly a quarter of all investor-State arbitrations have involved a Muslim-majority respondent State.[8]

---

4 Of course, the Muslim-majority world includes the Arab world only from a geopolitical standpoint. There are many Arabs who are either irreligious or observe faiths other than Islam.

5 This statistic is calculated using data gathered from the World Bank Data Center. *See generally* "Population – Total," World Bank Data Center, https://data.worldbank.org/indicator/SP.POP.TOTL.

6 This statistic is calculated using data gathered from the World Bank Data Center. *See generally* "GDP-PPP (current international $)," World Bank Data Center, https://data.worldbank.org/indicator/NY.GDP.MKTP.PP.CD.

7 U.S. Energy Information Administration, Production Data on Petroleum and Other Liquids, https://www.eia.gov/international/data/world/petroleum-and-other-liquids/annual-petroleum-and-other-liquids-production.

8 This statistic is calculated using data gathered from UNCTAD Investment Dispute Settlement Navigator. *See generally* "Known treaty-based ISDS cases," Investment Dispute Settlement Navigator, UNCTAD, https://investmentpolicy.unctad.org/investment-dispute-settlement.

Only with this context can one appreciate the potential implications of the existence of two MITs that cover the majority of the Muslim world. Whether one accepts the view that international investment arbitration contributes to the establishment of a favorable investment climate and spurs economic development, or instead adopts a critical view of investor-State arbitration, the Unified Arab Agreement and the OIC Agreement are worthy of a deeper analysis than the sparse attention afforded them to date. This book seeks to contribute to the existing scholarship by providing a comparative analysis of the two treaties. Section 1 provides an introduction to investment protection in general. Sections 2 and 3 summarize the UAA and the OIC Agreement, respectively, providing a brief overview of the contracting States, examining the purpose and structure of the agreements, and identifying subsequent amendments (if any) to the agreements. Sections 4 and 5 provide overviews and brief comparative analyses of the jurisdictional requirements and the substantive protections, while Part 6 deals with the dispute resolution mechanisms under the two agreements.

1.1 *Investment Protection in International Law*

International law has long aspired to protect the financial and legal interests of individuals and corporate entities operating in foreign States.[9] Nonetheless, historically, foreign investors could not bring direct claims against a foreign State for breach of international law.[10] Rather, they were required to seek "diplomatic protection": to petition their own governments to adopt or "espouse" their claims against the foreign State.[11] In the 19th century, diplomatic protection often took the form of "gunboat diplomacy," where European and other Western powers would threaten to attack the State unless it addressed the grievances of their nationals.[12] While this practice became less common in the 20th century, the home States of investors still exercised diplomatic protection by applying other forms of pressure on States hosting the investments in question ("host States").[13]

---

9 ALAN REDFERN ET AL, *Redfern and Hunter on International Arbitration* (6th ed. 2015), 8.01.

10 REDFERN (2015) (*supra* n 9) 8.01.

11 REDFERN (2015) (*supra* n 9) 8.01.

12 REDFERN (2015) (*supra* n 9) 8.01 ("For example, when faced with Venezuela's default on its sovereign debt in 1902, the governments of Great Britain, Germany, and Italy sent warships to the Venezuelan coast to demand reparation for the losses incurred by their nationals").

13 REDFERN (2015) (*supra* n 9) 8.07.

The use of diplomatic protection to address investor grievances was generally considered to be unsatisfactory for all parties involved.[14] From the perspective of the host State, diplomatic protection offered an unfair advantage to investors from powerful States, who could force a host State to capitulate without any fair determination of whether it had actually breached its obligations under international law. For an investor's home State, diplomatic protection often pitted domestic political considerations (such as lobbying from the aggrieved investor) against diplomatic stability and the home State's relations with the host State. From the investor's perspective, any claim it had against a foreign State would likely go unpursued unless: (i) its home State was sufficiently powerful relative to the host State, and (ii) the investor was capable of exerting considerable influence on its own government.[15]

The international community sought to avoid diplomatic protection by creating international avenues to resolve disputes. Matters proceeded rapidly following World War II. For example, in 1965, the international community concluded the Convention on the Settlement of Investment Disputes between States and Nationals of Other States (the ICSID Convention), which has been ratified by 156 States as of September 2021.[16] The Convention created a new arbitral forum in which foreign investors and host States could resolve their disputes. States could consent to arbitration by means of an arbitration clause placed in a contract, in their own domestic legislation, or in a bilateral or multilateral treaty.[17] Bilateral or multilateral investment treaty provisions have proven to be the most prevalent means by which States have consented to arbitration with foreign investors.[18]

1.2 *Proliferation of Investment Agreements*

The number of concluded investment treaties saw steady growth until the mid-1980s, when States began to enter into bilateral investment treaties (BITs) en masse.[19] The number of BITs increased from 385 at the end of the 1980s to

---

14 *See generally* Christoph Schreuer, *Investment Protection and International Relations*, University of Vienna, *available at*: https://www.univie.ac.at/intlaw/wordpress/pdf/87_investment_protect.pdf (discussing the limitations of diplomatic protection for both investors and the state involved).

15 REDFERN (2015) (*supra* n 9) 8.07.

16 REDFERN (2015) (*supra* n 9) 8.08; ICSID, *List of Contracting States and Other Signatories of the Convention (as of September 3, 2021)*, https://icsid.worldbank.org/sites/default/files/documents/2021_Sep.ICSID.ENG.pdf.

17 REDFERN (2015) (*supra* n 9) 8.08.

18 REDFERN (2015) (*supra* n 9) 8.08.

19 REDFERN (2015) (*supra* n 9) 8.10–8.11.

a total of 2,860 by May 2022,[20] and the number of investor-State arbitrations has seen a corresponding rise. At the start of the 21st century, there had been just 44 known[21] cases.[22] That number had risen to 608 by 2014[23] and to 1190 as of December 2021.[24]

The dramatic growth of BITs led to the proliferation of multilateral investment treaties (MITs), often in the form of economic cooperation treaties containing "investment chapters" that provide for investor-State arbitration.[25] Well-known examples include the now terminated North American Free Trade Agreement (NAFTA) (1994),[26] the Energy Charter Treaty (ECT) (1998),[27] the Dominican Republic and Central America–United States Free Trade Agreement (DR-CAFTA) (2004),[28] and the Association of Southeast Asian Nations (ASEAN) Comprehensive Investment Agreement (2012).[29] Against this background, one can appreciate that the States concluding the Unified Arab Agreement and the OIC Agreement – which entered into force in 1981

20 *See* UNCTAD, World Investment Report (UN, 2015), http://unctad.org/en/PublicationsLibrary/wir2015_en.pdf; *see* UNCTAD, Investment Policy Hub: International Investment Agreements Navigator, https://investmentpolicy.unctad.org/international-investment-agreements.

21 The total number of investment arbitrations is unknown because some cases are entirely confidential.

22 *See* UNCTAD, *Recent Trends in IIAs and ISDS*, INTERNATIONAL INVESTMENT AGREEMENTS (IIA) ISSUES NOTES NO. 1 (2015), https://unctad.org/en/PublicationsLibrary/webdiaepcb2015d1_en.pdf.

23 *See* UNCTAD (*supra* n 22) p. 5.

24 The current number of known investor-State arbitrations is available on the UNCTAD Investment Policy Centre, https://investmentpolicy.unctad.org/.

25 REDFERN (2015) (*supra* n 9) 8.11.

26 North American Free Trade Agreement (NAFTA), Ch. 11 ('Investment'), signed on 17 December 1992, entered into force on 1 January 1994. On November 30, 2018, Canada, the United States, and Mexico signed a new trade agreement designed to replace NAFTA called as USMCA. Under the new agreement, Canada will withdraw its consent for investor-State arbitration, and the U.S. and Mexico have greatly reduced the scope of protections offered to investor Claimants. *See United States-Mexico-Canada Agreement*, Office of the United States Trade Representative, *available at* https://ustr.gov/trade-agreements/free-trade-agreements/united-states-mexico-canada-agreement.

27 Energy Charter Treaty (ECT), signed on 17 December 1994, entered into force on 16 April 1998. The ECT covers investments in the energy sector for investors of more than fifty State parties within the territory of those States.

28 Dominican Republic and Central America–United States Free Trade Agreement (DR-CAFTA), signed on 5 August 2004, entered into force between 2006 and 2009 in seven signatory countries. This agreement covers investments from investors from the United States, Costa Rica, El Salvador, Guatemala, Honduras, Nicaragua, and the Dominican Republic in the territory of these states.

29 Association of Southeast Asian Nations (ASEAN) Comprehensive Investment Agreement, Signed on 26 February 2009, entered into force on 29 March 2012.

and 1988, respectively – were at the vanguard of investor protection, as both agreements were concluded well before most BITs and MITs. These treaties were therefore some of the earliest treaties.

2 The Unified Arab Agreement

2.1 *Background*

After gaining independence, Arab countries enacted stringent laws regulating foreign investment in their territories.[30] These laws sought to strengthen and protect the States' newfound economic sovereignty,[31] and did not distinguish between Arab and non-Arab foreign capital.[32] In the period that followed, many Arab States began to desire a greater flow of foreign direct investment into their territories, while at the same time remaining skeptical of foreign intervention, particularly that of Western States and corporations.[33] Similar skepticism was not directed, however, toward capital originating from other Arab States.[34]

The Arab States reached a consensus around the idea that, by establishing a pan-Arab investment regime, they could consolidate and promote regional development without risking domination by foreign capital.[35] Towards that end, the Unified Arab Agreement was approved at the 11th Arab Summit Conference held in Amman, Jordan from November 25–27, 1980.[36] The UAA entered into force shortly thereafter on September 9, 1981.[37] The UAA

30 Ahmed Sharaf Eldin, *Legislative Stability and the Investment Climate: A Comment on the Unified Agreement for the Investment of Arab Capital in the Arab Countries*, 3(1) ICSID REV. – FOREIGN INVESTMENT L. J. 147, 149 (1988) ("Following their political independence, Arab countries enacted laws which purported to re-organize certain aspects of foreign investments on their territories, and in which they included a number of restrictions aimed at strengthening their newly acquired economic independence.").

31 Eldin (1988) (*supra* n 30) 149.

32 Eldin (1988) (*supra* n 30) 149.

33 Eldin (1988) (*supra* n 30) 150 ("Arab countries realized that investment relations among them could, on the basis of mutual benefits and national interests, play a basic role in consolidating their own development").

34 Eldin (1988) (*supra* n 30) 149 ("Soon these countries realized that their fears of a domination by foreigners over their national economy were not justified in respect to Arab capital").

35 ldin (1988) (*supra* n 30) 50.

36 Caline Mouawad & Lillian Khoury, *Investment Arbitration under Multilateral Treaties in the Middle East*, 3 BCDR INT'L ARB. REV. 243, 244 (2016).

37 League of Arab States, *Ratification of the Unified Agreement for the Investment of Arab Capital in the Arab States*, http://www.lasportal.org/ar/legalnetwork/Pages/agreements_details.aspx?RID=25. UNCTAD considers that all the Arab States, including the Comoros,

represented a substantial development in the Arab world's efforts to create a uniform investment regime, which until that point had consisted only of informal discussions regarding judicial cooperation. The scope of the treaty far exceeded mere cooperation by providing concrete protections that could be enforced via international arbitration.[38] At present, all 22 members of the League of Arab States (the "Arab League") have ratified the Agreement, except for the Comoros.[39]

2.2 *Purpose and Structure*

With "the aim of strengthening overall Arab development and Arab economic integration,"[40] the UAA seeks to promote inter-Arab investment by establishing standards for the treatment of Arab capital across host countries.[41] The UAA provides that "investment dealings between Arab States are an essential part of joint Arab economic action, the regulation of which will mobilize production and thus enhance joint development on the basis of reciprocal benefits and national interests."[42]

It further adds:

> [P]roviding a suitable investment climate to stimulate Arab economic resources in the field of joint Arab investment requires that legal investment regulations be drawn up in the context of a well-established, coherent and integrated legal system which seeks to facilitate the transfer and use of Arab capital within the Arab States in such a manner as to

ratified the UAA but this seems to be inaccurate as the Comoros is not included in the list of States ratifying the UAA on the website of the League of Arab States and not mentioned in the scholarly writings.

38 Mouawad and Khoury (*supra* n 36) 243.

39 League of Arab States, *Ratification of the Unified Agreement for the Investment of Arab Capital in the Arab States*, http://www.lasportal.org/ar/legalnetwork/Pages/agreements_details.aspx?RID=25. The Arab League's twenty-two members are: Algeria, Bahrain, Comoros, Djibouti, Egypt, Iraq, Jordan, Kuwait, Lebanon, Libya, Mauritania, Morocco, Oman, Palestine, Qatar, Saudi Arabia, Somalia, Sudan, Syria, Tunisia, the United Arab Emirates, and Yemen. There is some inconsistency in the literature as to whether Algeria has ratified the UAA. *Compare, e.g.*, Mouawad and Khoury (*supra* n 36) 245 ("[The Arab Investment Agreement] has been ratified by all member States of the Arab League, except Algeria and the Comoros"), *with* Walid Ben Hamida, *The Arab League's Difficult Path Towards a Greater Quality and Clarity of Regional Investment Law: the Amended Arab Investment Agreement of 2013 Enters into Force*, 8 J. INTL ARB. 5, 5 (2016) 5 ("All the Arab League members, except Comoros Island, ratified the 1980 Agreement").

40 Unified Arab Agreement (*supra* n 1).

41 Nassib G. Ziadé, *ICSID's Contribution to the Development of Investment Arbitration in the Arab World*, 23 ICSID REV – FOREIGN INVESTMENT L. J. 233, 246 (2008).

42 Unified Arab Agreement (*supra* n 1).

> further their development, freedom and progress and improve the living standard of their citizens.[43]

The UAA promotes regional cooperation and inter-Arab solidarity by creating an integrated legal system that extends to every investor the privileges and protections that host States afford their own citizens. During negotiations of the UAA, there were two main proposals: (i) a unified legal regime of detailed, strong investment protections that would apply directly in domestic courts; or (ii) a convention containing minimum protections that were directly enforceable through international arbitration.[44] The States opted for the latter option as a means of establishing uniform investment protection while still safeguarding sovereignty.[45] The agreement therefore sets out the essential principles applicable to investment within the Arab world, while leaving it to the individual member States to formulate most of the particular rules prescribed by these principles.[46] Specifically, Article 16 of the UAA encourages member States to provide additional privileges to Arab investments beyond the minimum treatment which the UAA prescribes.[47]

In further service of the member States' desire to maintain a degree of sovereignty over the regulation of foreign capital,[48] the UAA recognizes each member State's rights to take action required by "reasons of public interest or security,"[49] and contains a process by which States may suspend within their territory the application of certain of the UAA's articles and provisions.[50] However, in our view, such provision constitutes an escape clause and a back door for the member States to derogate from their UAA obligations and its provisions, particularly that the UAA does not set out objective and precise conditions and standards for such derogation.[51] In addition, the terms "public interest and security" are vague and imprecise concepts, and, as a result, they may be misused and abused to circumvent the UAA system and framework.[52]

---

43 Unified Arab Agreement (*supra* n 1).

44 Eldin (1988) (*supra* n 30) 150 ("On the whole there were two main trends, one which was to prepare a legal regime for investments in the form of a unified law applicable directly in Arab States and the other which was to prepare a more detailed Convention on the basis of the provisions of the previous agreements in force").

45 Eldin (1988) (*supra* n 30) 153.

46 Eldin (1988) (*supra* n 30) 151.

47 Unified Arab Agreement (*supra* n 1) Art. 14.

48 Eldin (1988) (*supra* n 30) 156–157.

49 Unified Arab Agreement (*supra* n 1) Art. 39.

50 Unified Arab Agreement (*supra* n 1) Art. 19.

51 Mohamed S. Abdel Wahab, *A Study on the Unified Agreement for the Investment of Arab Capital*, World Journal of Arbitration, 17 ¶ 7 (2013).

52 Abdel Wahab (*supra* n 51) 17 ¶ 7.

Due to these concerns, the amended UAA (as adopted in 2013) does not include such a provision; but it is noteworthy that the applicability and effectiveness of this amendment remains to be tested given that the majority of Arab States have not yet ratified same as discussed below.

The UAA is arranged in nine chapters. Chapter I defines the terms, including "investor," "capital," and "investment." Chapters II–V set out the standard of treatment for investors and the guarantees provided to them. Chapter VI provides for the creation of an Arab Investment Court (the "AIC"). The UAA also includes an annex on arbitration and conciliation, which constitutes an integral part of the treaty. The most salient provisions will be discussed in greater detail in Parts 4 and 5, below.

2.3 *Amendment*

On January 22, 2013, during the Arab Summit for Economic and Social Development, the Unified Arab Agreement was amended.[53] The amendments likely arose as a response to regional uncertainty that followed the Arab Spring, but they might also be attributable to other developments in international investment law.[54] The amended UAA entered into force on April 24, 2016, three months from the date of its ratification by five member States as per its Article 30.[55] This amended UAA is currently ratified by Iraq, Jordan, Kuwait, Morocco, Oman, Palestine, Qatar and Saudi Arabia.[56] However, it remains unratified by the majority of Arab States despite the League of Arab States' calls for ratification,[57] which led to a complex and undesirable situation where

---

53 Hamida (2016) (*supra* n 39) 5.

54 Mouawad & Khoury (*supra* n 36) 244.

55 Hamida (2016) (*supra* n 39) 5; League of Arab States, *Ratification by Morocco of the "Customs Cooperation Agreement", "Amended Unified Agreement for the Investment of Arab Capital in the Arab States", "Statue of the Arab Union for Natural Reserves"*, http://www.lasportal.org/ar/sectors/sectorhome/Pages/SectorActivitiesDetails.aspx?RID=1951&SID=4.

56 Hamida (2016) (*supra* n 39) 6.

57 *Secretary-General's Report on the Sectors and Departments' Achievements during the Year of 2015*, 43 and 108, http://www.lasportal.org/ar/secretarygeneral/Documents/%D8%AA%D9%82%D8%B1%D9%8A%D8%B1%20%D8%A7%D9%84%D8%A3%D9%85%D9%8A%D9%86%20%D8%A7%D9%84%D8%B9%D8%A7%D9%85.pdf; The General Secretariat of the Economic and Social Council, *The Economic and Social Council at the Ministerial Level Regular Session No. 96* (*Report and Decisions*), 20 (2015), http://www.lasportal.org/ar/councils/economicalsocialcouncil/Documents/%D8%AA%D9%82%D8%B1%D9%8A%D8%B1%20%D9%88%D9%82%D8%B1%D8%A7%D8%B1%D8%A7%D8%AA%20%D8%A7%D9%84%D8%AF%D9%88%D8%B1%D8%A9%2096%20%D9%84%D9%84%D9%85%D8%AC%D9%84%D8%B3%20%D8%A7%D9%84%D8%A7%D9%82%D8%AA%D8%B5%D8%A7%D8%AF%D9%8A%20%D9%88%D8%A7%D9%84%D8%A7%D8%AC%D8%AA%D9%85%D8%A7%D8%B9%D9%8A%20%D8%A7%D9%84%D8%AF%D9%88%D8%B1%D8%A9%2096.pdf;

old and new regimes of the very same treaty (i.e. UAA) co-exist. This gives rise to doubts as to the effectiveness and prospects of the amended UAA, especially that are discussions over the adoption of a further amendment or a new agreement for the investment of the Arab capital.[58] That said, the Economic and Social Council of the League of Arab States invited the member States to submit their comments on the amended UAA.[59]

As will be discussed below in the further detail, the amended version of the UAA provides greater protections to a wider swath of eligible investors. Specifically, the amended UAA includes a more expansive definition of "Arab Investor": to qualify, an investor need only hold 51% of the share capital as opposed to maintaining full ownership in an investment.[60] The amended UAA also includes a more expansive definition of "investment" by extending it to social development and not restricting it to economic development.[61] Furthermore, the amended UAA introduces a provision requiring fair and equitable treatment of investors and a most-favored-nation (MFN) clause, removes limitations on free transfer of capital by investors, and disposes of the obligation of investors "to refrain from any activity that might violate public order and morality or which might involve illegitimate gains."[62] In addition, the expropriation clause was re-drafted to include reference to the market value of the investment as guidance for the quantification of the compensation.[63]

The General Secretariat of the Economic and Social Council, *The Economic and Social Council's Regular Session No. 97, The Economic Committee, The Secretary-General's Report*, September 1, 2015, 17, http://www.lasportal.org/ar/councils/economicalsocialcouncil/PublishingImages/Lists/EconomicalCommittee/AllItems/%D8%AA%D9%82%D8%B1%D9%8A%D8%B1%20%D8%A7%D9%84%D8%A7%D9%85%D9%8A%D9%86%20%D8%A7%D9%84%D8%B9%D8%A7%D9%85.pdf.

58 Bahgat Abou El Nasr (Manager of the Economic Integration Department – League of Arab States), *The Necessity of the Expeditious Conclusion of the New Agreement for the Investment of Arab Capital*, March 2022, https://araa.sa/index.php?option=com_content&view=article&id=6017&catid=4529&Itemid=172; The Economic Arab International Journal, *A Third Arab Agreement on the Investment of Capital .. An Expected Meeting in Next September*, July 27, 2018, https://www.aleqt.com/2018/07/27/article_1426916.html.

59 The Economic Arab International Journal, *A Third Arab Agreement on the Investment of Capital ... An Expected Meeting in Next September*, July 27, 2018, https://www.aleqt.com/2018/07/27/article_1426916.html; Arab Chambers Union, Unified Agreement for the Investment of Arab Capital in the Arab States (Amended), May 2018, http://uac-org.org/ar/publications/edetails/70/الاتفاقية-الموحدة-لاستثمار-رؤوس-الأموال-7-9-أيار-2018.

60 Unified Agreement for the Investment of Arab Capital in the Arab States of 1980 as Amended on 16 September 2013 [hereinafter Unified Arab Agreement as Amended in 2013], Art. 1; Hamida (2016) (*supra* n 39) 5.

61 Unified Arab Agreement as Amended in 2013 (*supra* n 60), Art. 1.

62 Hamida (2016) (*supra* n 39) 5–6.

63 Unified Arab Agreement as Amended in 2013 (*supra* n 60), Art. 8.

3 The OIC Agreement

3.1 *Background*

The first Islamic Summit was called in September 1969 in response to the arson attack on the Al-Aqsa Mosque in Jerusalem, an Islamic holy shrine.[64] The attack evoked a sense of unity and solidarity among Muslim States.[65] The Summit was attended by the representatives of twenty-four States (plus representatives of Muslims from India and the Palestine Liberation Organization (PLO)), who decided that "cooperation and mutual assistance in economic" fields among Muslim countries was necessary.[66] Out of this summit, the Organisation of Islamic Cooperation (OIC) was born.

The OIC is the world's leading international Islamic organisation and is often referred to as "The United Nations of the Islamic world."[67] The organisation comprises 57 States and spans four continents.[68] The OIC is modeled after the United Nations and its sphere of operations is similarly diverse.[69] It works to promote peace and conflict resolution, protect the rights of minority communities, promote cultural exchange and education, and foster intra-OIC trade and investment.[70]

This last sphere of operation – promoting trade and investment – was a cornerstone of the OIC's founding goals.[71] This initial spirit of economic cooperation resulted in the OIC Agreement on Investment, which was opened up for signature by Resolution No.7/12-E of the 12th Islamic Conference of Foreign Ministers, held in Baghdad from June 1–5, 1981.[72] It appears that the OIC Agreement entered into force in February of 1988, although there are conflicting

64 Mouawad & Khoury (*supra* n 36) 247; UNESCO, UNITED NATIONS EDUCATIONAL, SCIENTIFIC AND CULTURAL ORGANIZATION, BURNING OF THE AQSA MOSQUE, Eighty-Third Session of the Executive Board, Doc. 83 EX/34 (September 30, 1969), available at http://unesdoc.unesco.org/images/0019/001931/193149EB.pdf ("On 21 August 1969 the Aqsa Mosque, one of the three most venerated holy places of the Moslem work, was the victim of an act of criminal vandalism. The result was the collapse of a part of this historic monument and the destruction by fire of works of art of the greatest historic and cultural importance, not only to Moslem religious feeling but to world civilization and all mankind.").

65 Mouawad & Khoury (*supra* n 36) 247.

66 Mouawad & Khoury (*supra* n 36) 247.

67 *See* TURAN KAYOGLU, THE ORGANIZATION OF ISLAMIC COOPERATION: POLITICS, PROBLEMS, AND POTENTIAL (2015), 1.

68 KAYOGLU (2015) (*supra* n 67) 1.

69 KAYOGLU (2015) (*supra* n 67) 2.

70 KAYOGLU (2015) (*supra* n 67) 2.

71 Mouawad & Khoury (*supra* n 36) 247.

72 Mouawad & Khoury (*supra* n 36) 247.

accounts.[73] Of the 57 members of the OIC, 36 member States have signed the OIC Agreement and 29 have ratified it, making it the second-largest multilateral investment treaty in the world (after the ECT).[74]

3.2 *Purpose and Structure*

The Preamble of the OIC Agreement recognizes that investment relationships "are one of the major areas of economic cooperation" that will foster social and economic development "on the basis of common interest and mutual benefit[.]"[75] The main purpose of the Agreement is "to provide and develop a favorable climate for investments, in which the economic resources of the Islamic countries could circulate between them so that optimum utilization could be made of these resources in a way that will serve their development

---

73 Hossein Abedian & Reza Eftekhar, *Consent to Investor-State Arbitration in the Second Largest International Investment Protection Agreement: The Correct Interpretive Approach to Article 17 of the OIC Agreement*, 35(1) J. INTL ARB. 59, 60, fn 2 (2018); Franziska Tschofen, *Multilateral Approaches to the Treatment of Foreign Investment*, 7(2) ICSID REV. – FOR. INVESTMENT L. J. 384, 392 (1992) (explaining that Agreement "entered into force from date of ratification by 10 countries, on February 26, 1988."); Mouawad & Khoury (*supra* n 36) 254 (stating that Agreement entered into force on February 25, 1988); *but see* Scott Vesel, *Will the Future See More Investment Arbitrations Taking Place in the Middle East?*, 3(2) BCDR INTL ARB. REV. 267, 272 (2016) (the Agreement entered into force on September 23, 1986).

74 The following States have ratified the OIC Agreement: Burkina Faso, Cameroon, Egypt, Gabon, Gambia, Guinea, Indonesia, Iran, Iraq, Jordan, Kuwait, Lebanon, Libya, Mali, Morocco, Oman, Pakistan, Palestine, Qatar, Saudi Arabia, Senegal, Somalia, Sudan, Syria, Tajikistan, Tunisia, Turkey, Uganda, and the United Arab Emirates. See Craig D. Gaver, "*To the Centre": Itisaluna v. Iraq and ICSID's Entry into the OIC Debate*, Kluwer Arbitration Blog, 8 June 2020, http://arbitrationblog.kluwerarbitration.com/2020/06/08/to-the-centre-itisaluna-v-iraq-and-icsids-entry-into-the-oic-debate/; Yusuf Kumtepe, Riccardo Loschi (Columbia Law School), *Investment Dispute Settlement Body of the Organisation of Islamic Cooperation: A Dead End for Claims under the OIC Investment Agreement?*, Kluwer Arbitration Blog, 29 December 2019, http://arbitrationblog.kluwerarbitration.com/2019/12/29/investment-dispute-settlement-body-of-the-organisation-of-islamic-cooperation-a-dead-end-for-claims-under-the-oic-investment-agreement/; Mouawad & Khoury (supra n 36) fn 50; Dr. Mouhamadou Kane, *The Proposed OIC Investment Dispute Settlement Mechanism: A South-South Contribution to ISDS Reform*, CCSI Fall Speakers Series in International Investment Law and Policy, New York, 14 November 2019, slides of presentation available at https://ccsi.columbia.edu/sites/default/files/content/docs/events/Mouhamadou-Kane-PPT-presentation-Nov-14-2019.pdf.

75 OIC Agreement (*supra* n 2) Preamble; Hossein Abedian & Reza Eftekhar, *Consent to Investor-State Arbitration in the Second Largest International Investment Protection Agreement: The Correct Interpretive Approach to Article 17 of the OIC Investment Agreement*, 35(1) J. INTL ARB. 59 (2018).

and raise the standard of living of their peoples."[76] In essence, the OIC seeks to fortify relationships between its member States and to represent "the collective voice of the Muslim world."[77] OIC members have signed eight economic and trade cooperative agreements, of which the OIC Agreement is just one example.[78]

Despite the ambitious goals of the OIC Agreement, it lay dormant for three decades after it took effect.[79] It is one of the oldest and one of the largest multilateral investment treaties, but very few investors brought claims under the treaty until the 2010s.[80] Its period of dormancy might have two potential explanations.[81] First, the majority of investors from member States – and even the legal community at large – were unaware of the Agreement's existence.[82] The Agreement was not widely published; it was not even electronically available on the OIC website until 2009.[83] Second, some commentators have offered a cultural explanation, arguing that Islamic legal and business culture promotes the amicable settlement of investment disputes, as opposed to contentious processes such as arbitration.[84] The reality is that there is a significant number (93) of investment arbitrations between Muslim-majority host States and investors from other Muslim-majority States.[85]

The OIC Agreement contains four chapters and 25 articles. Like many investment agreements, Article 1 of the OIC Agreement defines key terms such as "investment" and "investor."[86] Articles 2 to 7 (Chapter 2) contain general provisions regarding promotion, facilitation, and stimulation of investments in the territory of State parties.[87] Article 8 (also in Chapter 2) contains an MFN clause.[88] Articles 10–16 (Chapter 3) outline the specific protections for

76 OIC Agreement (*supra* n 2) Preamble.

77 *History*, ORGANISATION OF ISLAMIC COOPERATION, https://www.oic-oci.org/page/?p_id=52&p_ref=26&lan=en, last accessed 24 February 2021.

78 Walid Ben Hamida, *A Fabulous Discovery: The Arbitration Offer Under the Organization of Islamic Cooperation Agreement Related to Investment*, J. INTL ARB. (2013) 638.

79 Hamida (2013) (*supra* n 78) 639.

80 Hamida (2013) (*supra* n 78) 639.

81 Hamida (2013) (*supra* n 78) 639.

82 Hamida (2013) (*supra* n 78) 639.

83 Hamida (2013) (*supra* n 78) 639.

84 Hamida (2013) (*supra* n 78) 639.

85 Statistic calculated using data gathered from UNCTAD Investment Policy Centre, https://investmentpolicy.unctad.org/.

86 OIC Agreement (*supra* n 2) Art. 1.

87 OIC Agreement (*supra* n 2) Arts. 2–7.

88 OIC Agreement (*supra* n 2) Art. 8.

investments: the duty not to expropriate (Article 10); free transfer of funds and capital (Article 11); free disposition of investments (Article 12); the investor's right to compensation (Article 13); the treatment of investors in emergency situations (Article 14); establishing an organisation for insurance and guarantee of investments (Article 15); and the duty to accord to investors effective rights for asserting claims, followed by a "fork-in-the-road" clause (Article 16) (this is discussed further below).[89] Article 17 is the dispute settlement clause which provides for conciliation and arbitration.[90] Articles 18–25 (Chapter 4) contain standard "general and final provisions" regulating, among other technical issues, the treaty's implementation.[91] The most important of these provisions will be discussed in greater detail in Parts 4 and 5, below.

3.3 *Proposed Amendment*

The OIC has proposed the establishment of an Investment Dispute Settlement Organ to provide a bespoke mechanism for investor-State arbitration among the OIC member States. The text of the proposal was not available at the time of this publication, but the OIC has appointed a "Project Manager," Dr. Mouhamadou Kane, who has publicly presented certain information regarding the proposal.[92]

The OIC's reform efforts aim to limit investor access to arbitration and to address concerns about transparency and arbitrator accountability.[93] The newly proposed procedures would require an aggrieved investor to take several intermediary steps before commencing investment arbitration proceedings.[94] An investor must first pursue its claims in the domestic courts of the host State.[95] After exhausting local remedies, the investor must appeal to its home State to amicably settle the issue with the host State.[96] If State-to-State talks fail, the investor may file a claim before a First Instance Panel, and the Panel's decision may be appealed before an Appellate Committee.[97] According to

89 OIC Agreement (*supra* n 2) Arts. 10–16.
90 OIC Agreement (*supra* n 2) Art. 17.
91 OIC Agreement (*supra* n 2) Arts. 18–25.
92 Kane (2019) (*supra* n 74).
93 Kumtepe (2019) (*supra* n 74).
94 Kumtepe (2019) (*supra* n 74), Slide 9.
95 Kumtepe (2019) (*supra* n 74), Slide 9.
96 Kumtepe (2019) (*supra* n 74), Slide 9.
97 Kumtepe (2019) (*supra* n 74), Slide 9.

Dr. Kane, the purpose of is to reduce the number of disputes brought against OIC member States.[98]

The draft protocol envisages several additional features that will strengthen respondent States' positions relative to investor claimants. Members of the First Instance Panel and the Appellate Committee would be appointed by OIC member States, a requirement that would deprive investors of their traditional role in selecting at least part of the arbitral tribunal.[99] In addition, the protocol establishes a separate policy forum, in which member States may agree to issue binding interpretations of the substantive provisions of the treaty.[100] The protocol also provides for the creation of an advisory center that will offer legal assistance to respondent States.[101] It was expected that the OIC member States would vote on the proposal in 2020.[102] In light of the COVID-19 pandemic in 2020, however, the exact status of the proposal is not clear.

This proposal reflects the increasingly popular idea that regional blocs – or even the international community more generally – should create a standing investment court. The most developed of these proposals is found in the Comprehensive Economic and Trade Agreement (CETA) between the European Union and Canada.[103] CETA establishes a standing investment tribunal composed of fifteen members which, like the members of the proposed OIC First Instance Panel and the Appellate Committee, would be selected by the treaty parties.[104] That is, investor claimants would no longer partake in the process of composing an arbitral tribunal. In theory, however, the State parties might have competing incentives, between protecting their interests as respondent states and the interests of their own nationals as potential future investor claimants, leading to a balanced roster of judges.[105]

• • •

98 Kumtepe (2019) (*supra* n 74), Slides 7 and 13.

99 Kumtepe (2019) (*supra* n 74).

100 Kumtepe (2019) (*supra* n 74), Slide 13.

101 Kumtepe (2019) (*supra* n 74), Slide 13.

102 Kumtepe (2019) (*supra* n 74).

103 Comprehensive Economic and Trade Agreement (CETA) between Canada and the EU and Its Member states, final text 29 February 2016, signed 30 October 2017, provisionally in force 21 September 2017.

104 *Id.* at art. 8.27.

105 *See* Sergio Puig & Gregory Shaffer, *Imperfect Alternatives: Institutional Choice and the Reform of Investment Law*, 112(3) AM. J. INT'L L. 361, 400 (2018).

Before turning to the jurisdictional requirements and substantive provisions of the two agreements, the following table summarizes and compares their current status and stated purpose.

TABLE 1 List of contracting States, preamble and amendments (if any) for the Unified Arab Agreement and the OIC Agreement

Criteria	Unified Arab Agreement	OIC Agreement
Contracting States	The UAA (as adopted in 1981) is ratified by all member States of the Arab League[106] except Comoros. However, the amended UAA of 2013 is currently ratified by Iraq, Jordan, Kuwait, Morocco, Oman, Palestine, Qatar and Saudi Arabia.	Of the fifty-seven different members of the OIC,[107] twenty-nine – Burkina Faso, Cameroon, Egypt, Gabon, Gambia, Guinea, Indonesia, Iran, Iraq, Jordan, Kuwait, Lebanon, Libya, Mali, Morocco, Oman, Pakistan, Palestine, Qatar, Saudi Arabia, Senegal, Somalia, Sudan, Syria, Tajikistan, Tunisia, Turkey, Uganda and the United Arab Emirates – have ratified the OIC Agreement. In addition, seven member States have signed the Agreement without ratifying.

106 Algeria, Bahrain, Comoros, Djibouti, Egypt, Iraq, Jordan, Kuwait, Lebanon, Libyan Arab Jamahiriya, Mauritania, Oman, Palestine, Qatar, Saudi Arabia, Syrian Arab Republic, Somalia, Sudan, Tunisia, The United Arab Emirates, and Yemen.

107 Afghanistan, Albania, Algeria, Azerbaijan, Bahrain, Bangladesh, Benin, Brunei Darussalam, Burkina Faso, Cameroon, Chad, Comoros, Djibouti, Egypt, Gabon, Gambia, Guinea, Guinea-Bissau, Indonesia, Islamic Republic of Iran, Iraq, Jordan, Kuwait, Kyrgyzstan, Lebanon, Libyan Arab Jamahiriya, Maldives, Malaysia, Mali, Mauritania, Morocco, Mozambique, Niger, Nigeria, Oman, Pakistan, Palestine, Qatar, Saudi Arabia, Senegal, Sierra Leone, Somalia, Sudan, Syrian Arab Republic, Tajikistan, Tunisia, Turkey, Turkmenistan, Uganda, United Arab Emirates, Yemen, and United Republic of Tanzania.

TABLE 1 List of contracting States, preamble and amendments (*cont.*)

Criteria	Unified Arab Agreement	OIC Agreement
Purpose, as Stated in Preamble	"[I]nvestment dealings between Arab States are an essential part of joint Arab economic action, the regulation of which will mobilize production and thus enhance joint development on the basis of reciprocal benefits and national interests." "[P]roviding a suitable investment climate to stimulate Arab economic resources in the field of joint Arab investment requires that legal investment regulations be drawn up in the context of a well-established, coherent and integrated legal system which seeks to facilitate the transfer and use of Arab capital within the Arab States in such a manner as to further their development, freedom and progress and improve the living standard of their citizens."	The Parties endeavour "to avail of the economic resources and potentialities available therein and to mobilize and utilize them in the best possible manner, within the framework of close cooperation among Member States," and are "Anxious to provide and develop a favourable climate for investments, in which the economic resources of the Islamic countries could circulate between them so that optimum utilization could be made of these resources in a way that will serve their development and raise the standard of living of their peoples."
Amendment	Three principal amendments were adopted on January 22, 2013: (1) a more expansive definition of "Arab Investor," which requires that the investor hold only 51% of the share capital as opposed to maintaining full ownership;	No amendment, though a draft amendment has been proposed.

TABLE 1 List of contracting States, preamble and amendments (*cont.*)

Criteria	Unified Arab Agreement	OIC Agreement
	(2) the addition of a fair and equitable treatment provision, complemented by the removal of limitations on free transfer of capital and prohibitions on actions in violation of public order and morality; and (3) a new dispute resolution option, which allows for a claim to be filed in a host country's domestic court system in circumstances in which the Arab Investment Court would otherwise have jurisdiction. Only Iraq, Jordan, Kuwait, Oman, and Palestine have ratified these amendments.	

4 Jurisdictional Requirements

In this Section, we provide a brief overview of the jurisdictional requirements of jurisdiction in international investment law, paying particular attention to the definitions of "investor" and "investment." It provides a comparative analysis of how the Unified Arab Agreement and the OIC Agreement define these two terms and discuss other jurisdictional issues that have arisen under the treaties.

4.1 *Investor*

An investor may submit a dispute to an arbitral tribunal only if that tribunal possesses jurisdiction over the dispute. First, the investor must identify an applicable treaty between its home State and the State in which the investment was made.[108] Second, if such a treaty exists, the investor must then typically

108 REDFERN (2015) (*supra* n 9) 8.14.

demonstrate that the alleged breach took place after the treaty took effect, since investment treaties do not always give retroactive effect to breaches that occurred prior to ratification.[109] The typical investment treaty does, however, protect investments that were made before the treaty was concluded.[110]

Next, the investor must demonstrate that it qualifies as an "investor" within the meaning of the term as defined by the treaty. The typical investment treaty extends protection both to natural persons and legal entities.[111] Investment treaties generally define the nationality of a natural person by reference to the domestic laws of the respective State parties.[112] Such an approach reflects a desire to defer to the authority of States to determine the criteria for identifying their own nationals.[113]

For natural persons, an issue may arise where the investor is a national of both the home State and the host State.[114] The ICSID Convention precludes such investors from bringing claims against the host State.[115] When considering this preclusion, some tribunals have looked to an investor's formal nationality, as opposed to an investor's "effective" or "dominant" nationality.[116] Other arbitral rules may not include a preclusion, but the relevant treaty may include an express prohibition on this point.[117]

With respect to legal entities, most investment treaties simply require that an entity be incorporated or constituted under the laws of the home State party.[118] Certain treaties contain additional requirements, such as that the investor must carry out business activities in the home State or else have its seat or *siege social* in the home State.[119]

---

109 REDFERN (2015) (*supra* n 9) 8.15.

110 REDFERN (2015) (*supra* n 9) 8.15.

111 REDFERN (2015) (*supra* n 9) 8.17.

112 REDFERN (2015) (*supra* n 9) 8.18.

113 REDFERN (2015) (*supra* n 9) 8.18.

114 REDFERN (2015) (*supra* n 9) 8.19.

115 Convention on the Settlement of Investment Disputes Between States and Nationals of Other States Art. 25(2)(a), Mar. 18, 1965, 17 U.S.T. 1270, 575 U.N.T.S. 159 [*hereinafter* ICSID Convention].

116 *See* REDFERN (2015) (*supra* n 9) 8.19; *Ioan Micula and others v. Romania*, ICSID Case No. ARB/05/20, Decision on Jurisdiction and Admissibility, 24 September 2008, ¶ 101; *Waguih Elie George Siag and Clorinda Vecchi v. The Arab Republic of Egypt*, ICSID Case No. ARB/05/15, Decision on Jurisdiction, 11 April 2007, ¶¶ 198–201.

117 REDFERN (2015) (*supra* n 9) 8.19.

118 REDFERN (2015) (*supra* n 9) 8.20.

119 *See, e.g.*, Agreement on Encouragement and Reciprocal Protection of Investments between the Kingdom of the Netherlands and the Argentine Republic, signed on 20 October 1992, entered into force on 1 October 1994, Art. 1(b) (protecting "legal persons constituted under

Most investment treaties extend protection to legal entities that are nationals of the host State but that are controlled by nationals of another State party.[120] The ICSID Convention expressly permits such an extension:

> National of another Contracting state means: ... any juridical person which had the nationality of the Contracting state party to the dispute ... and which, because of foreign control, the parties have agreed should be treated as a national of another Contracting state for the purposes of this Convention.[121]

This provision is significant because it is often advantageous, or even necessary, for foreign investors to incorporate a local entity.[122] Such entities may bring claims relating to direct losses.[123]

4.1.1 The Unified Arab Agreement

Article 1.7 of the Unified Arab Agreement (as adopted in 1981)[124] defines "Arab investor" as "an Arab citizen who owns Arab capital which he invests in the territory of a State Party of which he is not a national."[125] The definition of "Arab citizen" provided in Article 1.4 includes both natural and legal persons, provided the legal persons are fully owned, directly or indirectly, by citizens holding the nationality of one of the Arab States members of the Arab League. Arab States and State-owned entities are also considered "Arab citizens" under Article 1.4.[126] The extension of investor protections to Arab States is a reflection of the significant public investments in sectors like oil and gas.[127]

---

the law of that Contracting Party and actually doing business under the laws in force in any part of the territory of that Contracting Party in which a place of effective management is situated").

120 Redfern (2015) (*supra* n 9) 8.26.

121 ICSID Convention (*supra* n 115) Art. 25(2)(b).

122 Redfern (2015) (*supra* n 9) 8.27.

123 Redfern (2015) (*supra* n 9) 8.27.

124 The 2013 Amendment to the Unified Arab Agreement altered the numbering of many provisions; while the text will refer to the original agreement, the location in the amended agreement will be noted in the footnotes.

125 Unified Arab Agreement (*supra* n 1) Art. 1.7; *see also* Unified Arab Agreement as Amended in 2013 (*supra* n 60) Art. 1.8.

126 Unified Arab Agreement (*supra* n 1) Art. 1.4.

127 Mouawad & Khoury (*supra* n 36) 244 fn 19 ("Prominent examples include the Saudi Arabian Oil Company (Saudi Aramco) and the Kuwait Petroleum Corporation, both State-owned entities that manage the hydrocarbon interests of their respective States throughout the world."). *See also* Walid Ben Hamida, 'The First Arab Investment Court

It is thus clear that the UAA (as adopted in 1981) adopts a narrow definition of the "Arab investor" by restricting the agreement's protection to the investors with exclusively Arab capital.[128] However, when the UAA was amended in 2013, the term "investor" was also amended to include a natural or legal person owning Arab capital provided that the investor holds directly at least 51% of the share capital of the relevant legal persons.[129] Therefore, in the States that have adopted the 2013 amendments, only a 51% majority Arab-citizen ownership (or more) is required for a legal person to qualify as an investor under the UAA (as amended in 2013). As to the remaining Arab States, which have not ratified the UAA amendments of 2013, they still require that the legal person be fully owned by an Arab citizen in order to qualify as an investor under the UAA (as adopted in 1981) and to benefit the protection provided thereunder.

4.1.2 The OIC Agreement

Article 1.6 of the OIC Agreement defines "investor" to include "[t]he Government of any contracting party or natural corporate person, who is a national of a contracting party and who owns the capital and invests it in the territory of another contracting party."[130]

The Agreement defines "natural person" as "[a]ny individual enjoying the nationality of a contracting party according to the provisions of the nationality law in force therein," while it defines "Legal Personality" as "[a]ny entity established in accordance with the laws in force in any contracting party and recognized by the law under which its legal personality is established."[131] The definition is broad, encompassing natural persons, State entities, and legal entities that are established and recognized under the laws of a contracting party. Since there are no limitations on the definition of "legal persons," subsidiaries of non-contracting parent companies may fall within the scope of the definition, provided, however, that the subsidiaries are incorporated in the contracting State.[132]

Decision', (2006) 7 JWIT 699, 702. A more recent case based on the protection afforded to State-owned entities (albeit under a different investment agreement) is *State General Reserve Fund of the Sultanate of Oman v. Republic of Bulgaria*, ICSID Case No. ARB/15/43, Award, 13 August 2019.

128 Abdel Wahab (*supra* n 51) 23 ¶ 25.

129 Unified Arab Agreement as Amended in 2013 (*supra* n 60) Art. 1.8.

130 OIC Agreement (*supra* n 2) Art. 1.6.

131 OIC Agreement (*supra* n 2) Art. 1.6(a) and (b).

132 Mouawad & Khoury (*supra* n 36) 247 ("Importantly, this definition imposes no requirements on the owners of a legal person, suggesting that the Agreement may apply to

4.1.3 Comparison of the Agreements

The OIC Agreement offers broader definitions of 'investor' and 'investment' than the Unified Arab Agreement, and thus its jurisdictional scope is less restrictive. Like the UAA, the OIC Agreement defines 'investors' to include natural persons, State parties, and legal entities. But unlike the UAA, the OIC Agreement does not impose restrictive ownership criteria on legal entities. Instead, it applies to any legal entity that is established and recognized by the laws of a contracting party.[133]

TABLE 2 Definition of "investor" in the OIC Agreement, the Unified Arab Agreement, and the 2013 amendments to the Unified Arab Agreement

OIC Agreement	Unified Arab Agreement (1981)	Unified Arab Agreement (2013 Amendment)
The Government of any contracting party or natural corporate person, who is a national of a contracting party and who owns the capital and invests it in the territory of another contracting party. Nationality shall be determined as follows: (a) *Natural Person*: Any individual enjoying the nationality of a contracting party according to the provisions of the nationality law in force therein.	[A]n Arab citizen who owns Arab capital which he invests in the territory of a State Party of which he is not a national[.] (Article 1.7) (where "Arab citizen" means "[A]n individual or a body corporate having the nationality of a State Party, provided that no part of the capital of such body corporate belongs either directly or indirectly to non-Arab citizens. Joint Arab projects which are fully	The natural or juridical person who/which owns Arab capital which it invests in the territory of a State Party of which it is not a national, provided that the Arab investor holds directly at least (51%) of the share capital of the relevant juridical person. (Article 1.8)

subsidiaries of non-contracting party parent companies, so long as these subsidiaries are incorporated in contracting States").

133 OIC Agreement (*supra* n 2), Art. 1.6(b).

TABLE 2 Definition of "investor" in the OIC Agreement (*cont.*)

OIC Agreement	Unified Arab Agreement (1981)	Unified Arab Agreement (2013 Amendment)
(b) *Legal Personality*: Any entity established in accordance with the laws in force in any contracting party and recognized by the law under which its legal personality is established. (Article 1.6)	owned by Arab citizens shall be deemed to be included within this definition in instances where they do not have the nationality of another State[.]" (Article 1.4)	

4.2 *Investments*

A qualifying investor must next demonstrate that it has made a protected "investment" within the meaning of the relevant treaty.[134] Most investment treaties contain a broad definition of "investment," often referring to "every kind of asset" or "every kind of investment in the territory" of the host State.[135] The typical treaty will then include a non-exhaustive list of example investments.[136]

Many treaties define investment to include a shareholding in an entity established in the host State.[137] Furthermore, an indirect shareholding via one or more intermediary companies may constitute a protected investment, even when the treaty's definition of "investment" does not expressly include

134 *See* UNCTAD, *Scope and Definitions* (*A Sequel*), SERIES ON ISSUES IN INTERNATIONAL INVESTMENT AGREEMENTS No. 2 (2011).

135 REDFERN (2015) (*supra* n 9) 8.28.

136 REDFERN (2015) (*supra* n 9) 8.28. *See, e.g.*, Agreement between the Government of the United Kingdom of Great Britain and Northern Ireland and the Government of Chile for the Promotion and Protection of Investments, signed on 8 January 1996, entered into force on 21 April 1997, Art. 1(a) ("investment means every kind of asset and in particular, though not exclusively, includes: (i) movable and immovable property and any other property rights such as mortgages, liens and pledges; (ii) shares in, and stock and debentures of a company, and any other form of participation in a company; (iii) claims to money or to any performance under contract having a financial value; (iv) intellectual property rights, goodwill, technical processes and know-how; (v) business concessions conferred by law or under contract, including concessions to search for, cultivate or extract or exploitation of natural resources").

137 REDFERN (2015) (*supra* n 9) 8.30.

"indirect" investments.[138] The *Siemens v. Argentina* tribunal observed that the definition of "investment" is broad and that the "Treaty does not require that there be no interposed companies between the investment and the ultimate owner of the company."[139] Similarly, in *Tza Yap Shum v. Peru*, the tribunal found that a Chinese investor's shareholding in a British Virgin Islands company, which in turn held shares in a local Peruvian company, constituted a protected investment under the Peru–China BIT.[140] Tribunals have noted there may be a limit to "indirectness" of the investment but they have not identified what this limit would be.[141]

Several tribunals, pointing to the ICSID Convention, and therefore apply a "double barrel" or "double keyhole test." Here, an investment must not only meet the definition of "investment" in the relevant treaty, but must also satisfy an objective definition of "investment."[142] These tribunals have cited Article 25 of the ICSID Convention, which provides that legal disputes arise

138 *See, e.g., Mobil Corporation v. Bolivarian Republic of Venezuela*, ICSID Case No. ARB/07/27, Decision on Jurisiction, 10 June 2010, ¶ 165.

139 *Siemens A.G. v. Argentine Republic*, ICSID Case No. ARB/02/8, Decision on Jurisdiction, 3 August 2004, ¶ 137. *See also National Grid P.L.C. v. Argentina Republic*, UNCITRAL, Award, 3 November 2008, ¶ 126 ("The actual issue raised by the Respondent is whether indirect investments are eligible as protected investments under the Treaty. The structure of the investment shows that the Claimant channeled its investment in the Argentine Republic through seven companies 100% owned by the Claimant and not necessarily British companies. The Treaty definition of investment encompasses direct and indirect investments and, therefore, for the purpose of ascertaining which British investor ultimately qualifies for protection under the Treaty, there is no difference between an investment made by Citelec and one made through Transener for purposes of protection of the ultimate British investor under the Treaty.").

140 *Sr Tza Yap Shum v. Republic of Peru*, Decision on Jurisdiction and Competence, ICSID Case No. ARB/07/6, 19 June 2009, ¶ 111.

141 *See, e.g., Enron Creditors Recovery Corporation (formerly Enron Corporation) and Ponderosa Assets, L.P. v. Argentine Republic*, ICSID Case No. ARB/01/3, Decision on Jurisdiction, 14 January 2004,¶ 52 ("The Tribunal notes that while investors can claim in their own right under the provisions of the treaty, there is indeed a need to establish a cut-off point beyond which claims would not be permissible as they would have only a remote connection to the affected company. As this is in essence a question of admissibility of claims, the answer lies in establishing the extent of the consent to arbitration of the host State. If consent has been given in respect of an investor and an investment, it can be reasonably concluded that the claims brought by such investor are admissible under the treaty. If the consent cannot be considered as extending to another investor or investment, these other claims should then be considered inadmissible as being only remotely connected with the affected company and the scope of the legal system protecting that investment.").

142 REDFERN (2015) (*supra* n 9) 8.39. *See also Malicorp Limited v. Arab Republic of Egypt*, ICSID Case No. ARB/08/18, Award, 7 February 2011, ¶ 107 ("Even though the point is not undisputed, in order for a proceeding based on breach of a treaty to be admissible, the

directly out of an "investment."[143] While the Convention does not define the term "investment," tribunals have developed an inherent meaning for the term "investment" under the ICSID Convention.[144] To illustrate these limits, it is often argued that a simple contract for the sale of goods could not qualify as an investment under Article 25.[145] These tribunals have held that an investment must involve "a certain duration, a certain regularity of profit and return, assumption of risk, a substantial commitment and a significance for the host State's development,"[146] although there is significant disagreement whether (and to what extent) investments must contribute to the host State's development.[147] For example, the tribunal in *Saba Fakes v. Turkey* found that, while economic development is a proclaimed objective of the ICSID Convention, it is not an independent criterion for the definition of "investment."[148]

The objective notion of "investment" has been applied outside the ICSID context, for example, in *Romak v. Uzbekistan*, a case conducted under the UNCITRAL rules.[149] The tribunal invoked the "inherent meaning" of the term "investments" under the BIT, which the tribunal found to include a "contribution

---

investment to which the dispute relates must pass a double test (also known as the 'double keyhole approach' or 'double-barrelled test." It must in practice correspond:
- on the one hand, to the meaning given to the term by the treaty, which defines the framework of the consent given by the State, and also
- on the other, to the meaning given in the ICSID Convention, which determines the jurisdiction of the Centre and the arbitral tribunals acting under its auspices.") (internal citations omitted).

143 ICSID Convention (*supra* n 115) Art. 25.

144 SCHREUER ET AL, THE ICSID CONVENTION: A COMMENTARY (2001), 83. *See also Generation Ukraine Inc. v. Ukraine*, ICSID Case No. ARB/00/9, Final Award, 16 September 2003, ¶ 8.2("No definition of 'investment' is to be found in the ICSID Convention. It is well settled that Contracting Parties may agree upon a more precise definition of 'investment' in a separate legal instrument.").

145 *See, e.g., SGS Société Générale de Surveillance SA v. Republic of Paraguay*, ICSID Case No. ARB/07/29, Decision on Jurisdiction, 12 February 2010, ¶ 93.

146 *See, e.g., Salini Costruttori SpA and Italstrade SpA v. Morocco*, ICSID Case No. ARB/00/4, Decision on Jurisdiction, 31 July 2001, ¶¶ 50–57.

147 *See, e.g., LESI SpA and ASTALDI SpA v. People's Democratic Republic of Algeria Award*, ICSID Case No. ARB/05/3, 12 July 2006, ¶ 72; *Mr Saba Fakes v. Republic of Turkey*, Award, ICSID Case No. ARB/07/20, 12 July 2010, ¶ 111 ("The promotion and protection of investments in host States is expected to contribute to their economic development. Such development is an expected consequence, not a separate requirement, of the investment projects carried out by a number of investors in the aggregate").

148 *Mr Saba Fakes v. Republic of Turkey*, Award, ICSID Case No. ARB/07/20, 12 July 2010, ¶ 111.

149 *Romak SA (Switzerland) v. Republic of Uzbekistan*, PCA Case No. AA280, Award, 26 November 2009, ¶ 207.

that extends over a *certain period of time* and involves some *risk*."[150] This decision was, however, criticized in *Guaracachi v. Bolivia*, in which the tribunal opined:

> It is not appropriate to import 'objective' definitions of investment ... in the context of a non-ICSID arbitration such as the present case. On the contrary, the definition of protected investment, at least in non-ICSID arbitrations, is to be obtained only from the (very broad) definition contained in the BIT ..."[151]

4.2.1 The Unified Arab Agreement

Article 1.6 of the Unified Arab Agreement defines "Investment of Arab Capital"[152] as "the use of Arab capital in a field of economic development with a view to obtaining a return in the territory of a State Party other than the State of which the Arab investor is a national or its transfer to a State Party for such purpose in accordance with the provisions of this Agreement...."[153] Accordingly, the UAA (as adopted in 1981) adopts a narrow definition of the "investment" by restricting it to the capital used in an economic development filed and for the purpose of obtaining a return.[154] This definition is in line with the definition followed in the ICSID case of *Salini v. Morocco* which defines the "investment" from an economic perspective requiring it to be subject to a financial risk and to contribute in the economic development of the host State.[155]

In the 2013 amendment of the UAA, the term "Investment of Arab Capital" was broadened. The amended definition of "Investment of Arab Capital" includes Arab capital deployed not only in "a field of economic development," but also in a "social field," suggesting a possible expansion in the protected spheres of

150 *Romak SA (Switzerland) v. Republic of Uzbekistan*, PCA Case No. AA280, Award, 26 November 2009, ¶ 207 (emphasis in original).

151 *Guaracachi America Inc. and Rurelec Plc v. Plurinational State of Bolivia*, PCA Case No. 2011–17, Award, 31 January 2014, ¶ 364.

152 Unified Arab Agreement (*supra* n 1) Art. 1.6. Art. 1.5 defines "Arab Capital" as "assets owned by an Arab citizen comprising any material and immaterial rights which have a cash valuation, including bank deposits and financial investments. Revenues accruing from Arab assets shall be regarded as Arab assets, as shall any joint share to which this definition applies."

153 Unified Arab Agreement (*supra* n 1) Art. 1.6.

154 Abdel Wahab (*supra* n 51) 20 ¶ 17.

155 Salini Costruttori S.p.A. and Italstrade S.p.A. v. Kingdom of Morocco, Decision on Jurisdiction, 31 July 2001, ¶ 52–57.

investment.[156] The agreement, however, does not expound on the term "social field."

4.2.2 The OIC Agreement

Article 1.5 of the OIC Agreement defines "investment" as "[t]he employment of capital in one of the permissible fields in the territories of a contracting party with a view to achieving a profitable return, or the transfer of capital to a contracting party for the same purpose, in accordance with this Agreement."[157]

Article 1.4 of the OIC Agreement defines "capital" as any asset or thing that "can be evaluated in monetary terms" and is "owned by a contracting party to this Agreement or by its nationals," whether the asset or thing is "movable, immovable, in cash, in kind, [or] tangible ... and shall include the net profits accruing from such assets and the undivided shares and intangible rights."

4.2.3 Comparison of the Agreements

The meaning of "investment" appears to be broader under the OIC Agreement. While Article 1.6 of the Unified Arab Agreement (as adopted in 1981) defines "investment" in the context of a "field of economic development,"[158] Article 1.5 of the OIC Agreement defines it in the context of "one of the permissible fields in the territories of a contracting party."[159] Although the "permissible" language might seem narrower at first glance, the tribunal in *Al-Warraq v. Indonesia* held that "there is no explicit reference to direct or indirect investments in the OIC Agreement, and in particular in Article 1(4) and 1(5)," and Article 1(4) "does not require the shares to be owned personally or directly, leaving open the possibility of ownership through an investment vehicle,"[160] thereby potentially extending the scope to offer far-reaching economic protection.[161] Accordingly,

---

156 Unified Arab Agreement as Amended in 2013 (*supra* n 60) Art. 1.7.

157 OIC Agreement (*supra* n 2) Art 1.5.

158 Unified Arab Agreement (*supra* n 1) Art. 1.6.

159 OIC Agreement (*supra* n 2) Art 1.5.

160 *Hesham Talaat M. Al-Warraq v. Republic of Indonesia*, UNCITRAL, Final Award, 15 December 2014, ¶ 503 ('Article 1(5) requires the "employment" of capital in the territory of a contracting party (here Indonesia) without designating that the employment must be in the investor's own name. Similarly Article 1(4), which defines capital, requires the assets (here the shares in Bank Century) to be "owned" by a national of a contracting State (here, allegedly the claimant, a national of Saudi Arabia) but does not require the shares to be owned personally or directly, leaving open the possibility of ownership through an investment vehicle such as FGAH').

161 Peter Rosher, Multilateral Investment Protection Agreements in the Middle East and North Africa: Two Little Known but Promising Instruments, FRENCH INTL ARB. REV.

unlike the UAA, the OIC Agreement does not require that the investment contributes to the economic development of the host State. However, it is noteworthy that the UAA amendment of 2013 extends the definition of investment to the capital deployed not only for economic development but also for social purposes.[162]

In defining "investment," the OIC Agreement refers to the use of the capital by the investor with a view to "achieving a *profitable* return."[163] In contrast, the Unified Arab Agreement refers simply to the employment of capital with a view to "obtaining a return."[164] The OIC Agreement seemingly has a qualifier to the use of the capital, that it be made with a view to achieve a return that is "profitable." While the additional word "profitable" used in the OIC agreement is not defined, it could, however, be interpreted to confine the scope of the word "investment" as used in the OIC Agreement.

TABLE 3 Meaning of "investment" in the OIC Agreement, the Unified Arab Agreement, and the 2013 amendments to the Unified Arab Agreement

OIC Agreement	**Unified Arab Agreement**	**Unified Arab Agreement (2013 Amendment)**
The employment of capital in one of the permissible fields in the territories of a contracting party with a view to achieving a profitable return, or the transfer of capital to a contracting party for the same purpose, in accordance with this Agreement. (Article 1.5)	[T]he use of Arab capital in a field of economic development with a view to obtaining a return in the territory of a State Party other than the State of which the Arab investor is a national or its transfer to a State Party for such purpose in accordance with the provisions of this Agreement[.] (Article 1.6)	The use of Arab capital in an economic or social field in the territory of a State Party other than the State of which the Arab investor is a national, or its transfer to said State with a view to obtaining a return in accordance with the provisions of this Agreement. (Article 1.7)

(2017), https://www.reedsmith.com/en/perspectives/2017/12/multilateral-investment-protection-agreements.

162 Unified Arab Agreement as Amended in 2013 (*supra* n 60) Art. 1.7.

163 OIC Agreement (*supra* n 2) Art 1.5.

164 Unified Arab Agreement (*supra* n 1) Art. 1.6.

4.3 *The OIC Agreement and Jurisdiction in the* Itisaluna Iraq et al. v. Iraq *Case Decided under the ICSID Convention*

For a long time, there were no disputes under the OIC Agreement and so the jurisdictional issues had not been tested. The OIC Agreement was successfully invoked, for the first time, in *Al Warraq v. Indonesia* case which was followed by other cases that are further discussed below.[165] With respect to the jurisdiction under the OIC Agreement, *Itisaluna Iraq et al. v. Iraq* is the first known case in which an ICSID tribunal has dealt with questions of interpretation and application of the OIC Agreement to determine whether it could properly exercise jurisdiction under Article 25(1) of the ICSID Convention.[166] The dispute involved a group of foreign telecom investors that brought suit under the OIC Agreement against Iraq for disrupting its commercial operations.[167] In an effort to establish ICSID's jurisdiction under Article 25(1), the claimants invoked Article 8 of the OIC Agreement, which contains a Most-Favored Nation (MFN) clause.[168] In theory, such a clause obliges a State to treat investors as well as it does the investors of any other State.[169] The claimants accordingly sought to use the MFN clause to "import" an ICSID arbitration clause found in the Iraq-Japan BIT, on the theory that Iraq's offer of arbitration to investors from Japan constituted "treatment" that should be afforded to the claimants as well.[170]

There is, however, a significant disagreement over the scope of MFN clauses, in particular regarding the question of whether they may be used to invoke *procedural* clauses – such as the ICSID arbitration clause in the Iraq-Japan BIT – in addition to *substantive* protections (such as a requirement that investors be treated fairly and equitably).[171] This controversy over the application of the MFN clause to procedural matters, and, in particular, to the dispute

165 Mouawad & Khoury (*supra* n 36) 254.

166 *See Itisaluna Iraq LLC, Munir Sukhtian International Investment LLC, VTEL Holdings Ltd., VTEL Middle* East *and Africa Limited v. Republic of Iraq*, ICSID Case No. ARB/17/10, Final Award, 3 April 2020.

167 Two of the claimants were Jordanian, while the other two were incorporated under the laws of Dubai. *Itisaluna* (*supra* n 166) ¶ 153.

168 *See* Section 5.4.2, *infra*.

169 Newcombe & Paradell (*supra* n 242) 193.

170 *See Itisaluna* (*supra* n 166) ¶¶ 20–21.

171 *See generally* Zachary Douglas, *The MFN Clause in Investment Arbitration: Treaty Interpretation Off the Rails*, 2 J. INT'L DISPUTE SETTLEMENT 97 (2010) (summarizing evolution of disagreement); *Chapter 5 – Most-Favoured-Nation Treatment*, in Andrew Newcombe and Lluís Paradell, Law and Practice of Investment Treaties: Standards of Treatment, Kluwer Law International (2009); Stephan W. Schill, *Chapter 18: Maffezini v. Plama: Reflections on the Jurisprudential Schism in the Application of Most-Favored-Nation Clauses to Matters of Dispute Settlement*, in Meg Kinnear, Geraldine R. Fischer, et al. (eds), Building International Investment Law: The First 50 Years of ICSID, Kluwer Law

resolution mechanisms, is also manifested in the inconsistent jurisprudence in relation to this issue which is further discussed below.

Back to *Itisaluna*, the claimants in this case argued that the imported arbitration clause established Iraq's consent to submit their dispute to ICSID, thereby satisfying the requirement of Article 25(1) that the "parties to the dispute consent in writing to submit [the dispute] to" ICSID (also known as the requirement of *ratione voluntatis*).[172] Iraq countered that the OIC Agreement, and in particular Article 17, does not provide for ICSID arbitration and that such consent cannot be imported from another treaty via the OIC Agreement's MFN clause.

As discussed below, the majority agreed with Iraq and declined jurisdiction on the basis that consent to ICSID arbitration could not be imported into the OIC Agreement.[173] The claimant-appointed arbitrator, however, dissented from the majority and argued that the MFN clause could operate to import consent to ICSID arbitration from another treaty.[174] (*See* discussion *infra* Part 5.4 on Article 8 Most Favored Nation clause.)

4.3.1 Majority Decision

While the majority made clear that the key question before the tribunal was whether an unrelated BIT could be incorporated into the OIC Agreement by operation of its MFN clause, it addressed the additional jurisdictional questions of (i) whether Articles 16[175] and 17[176] of the OIC Agreement provide for

---

International (2015); Alejandro López Ortiz, José Joaquín Caicedo, et al., *Two Solutions For One Problem: Latin America's Reactions to Concerns*, Wolters Kluwer España (2016).

172 ICSID Convention (*supra* n 115) Art. 25(1).

173 The majority was comprised of tribunal chair Daniel Bethlehem QC and the respondent's appointee, Bridgette Stern.

174 The dissent was authored by Wolfgang Peter.

175 Article 16 provides: "The host state undertakes to allow the investor the right to resort to its national judicial system to complain against a measure adopted by its authorities against him, or to contest the extent of its conformity with the provisions of the regulations and laws in force in its territory, or to complain against the non-adoption by the host state of a certain measure which is in the interest of the investor, and which the state should have adopted, irrespective of whether the complaint is related, or otherwise, to the implementation of the provisions of the Agreement to the relationship between the investor and the host state. Provided that if the investor chooses to raise the complaint before the national courts or before an arbitral tribunal then having done so before one of the two quarters he loses the right of recourse to the other."

176 Article 17 provides, in relevant part: "Until an Organ for the settlement of disputes arising under the Agreement is established, disputes that may arise shall be entitled through conciliation or arbitration in accordance with the following rules and procedures:
1. Conciliation

investor-State arbitration; (ii) whether an attempt at conciliation is a condition precedent to arbitration under the OIC Agreement; and (iii) whether the MFN clause can be interpreted to provide for importation of the written consent required by Article 25(1) of the ICSID Convention.

Scarce case law on the treaty's interpretation[177] and the need to preserve the treaty's multilateral character were important considerations under the tribunal's reasoning. The majority underscored the need for a cautious approach with respect to any interpretation of the OIC Agreement, acknowledging that in the absence of "clear dispositive practice of all its Contracting Parties," any interpretation which it might adopt "would invariably colour the appreciation of the legal obligations of other OIC Agreement Contracting Parties under the OIC Agreement."[178] The majority declined to refer to the treaty practice of OIC member States in other contexts, reasoning that the unrelated bilateral treaty practice of one State party "cannot be safely relied upon as a yardstick for the interpretation and application of [a] multilateral agreement."[179] In other words, the OIC Agreement "must carry the same meaning for all its Contracting Parties" and its meaning "cannot be shaped by the unrelated treaty practice of one Contracting Party only."[180] To hold otherwise would lead to the "fracturing of the multilateral character of a multilateral treaty."[181]

While the claimants argued that Articles 16 and 17 of the OIC Agreement must be read together to provide for investor-State arbitration, the respondent insisted that there was a clear distinction between the two articles.[182] Article 16, the respondent argued, addressed domestic dispute settlement modalities of

---

a. In case the parties to the dispute agree on conciliation, the agreement shall include a description of the dispute, the claims of the parties to the dispute and the name of the conciliator whom they have chosen [....]

2. Arbitration

a. If the two parties to the dispute do not reach an agreement as a result of their resort to conciliation, or if the conciliator is unable to issue his report within the prescribed period, or if the two parties do not accept the solutions proposed therein, then each party has the right to resort to the Arbitration Tribunal for a final decision on the dispute [....]"

177 The majority cited only one other UNCITRAL case, *Al-Warraq v. Indonesia*, which decided the OIC Agreement's MFN clause could import fair and equitable treatment protection from a bilateral investment treaty. The majority declined to apply parallel reasoning here. The *Itisaluna* tribunal appears not to have considered another 2016 UNCITRAL tribunal decision in *KCI v. Gabon*, which also accepted the importing of fair and equitable treatment protection through the OIC Agreement's MFN clause.

178 *Itisaluna* (*supra* n 166) ¶ 153.

179 *Itisaluna* (*supra* n 166) ¶ 153.

180 *Itisaluna* (*supra* n 166) ¶ 153.

181 *Itisaluna* (*supra* n 166) ¶ 154.

182 *Itisaluna* (*supra* n 166) ¶ 157.

the host State, and Article 17 addressed inter-State diplomatic proceedings, rather than investor-State proceedings. The majority sided with the claimants on this point and applied a holistic interpretation in reaching its conclusion that "Article 16 cannot be detached from Article 17."[183] Nor could these articles be read in isolation from the object and purpose of the Agreement "to provide and develop a favourable climate for investments."[184] Interpreted within this wider context, the majority found a strong indication that investor-State dispute settlement modalities were contemplated by the OIC Agreement. (*See* discussion *infra* Part 6.)

The majority held that Article 17(2)(a) of the OIC Agreement establishes a "right" for "each party" to resort to arbitration.[185] However, the majority interpreted Article 17 to require conciliation as a condition precedent for resort to arbitration based on the conditional "if … then" language:

> ***If*** the two parties to the dispute do not reach an agreement as a result of their resort to conciliation, ***or if*** the conciliator is unable to issue his report within the prescribed period, ***or if*** the two parties do not accept the solutions proposed therein, ***then*** each party has the right to resort to the Arbitration Tribunal for a final decision on the dispute. (*Emphasis in original decision.*)[186]

The majority observed that this interpretation was consistent with the well-established practice in international investment agreements to predicate consent to arbitration on the prior participation in "consultations" or non-binding dispute settlement procedures. According to the majority, the treaty's reference to "each party" presumes the possibility of proceedings not only against a State party, but also against an investor party. Thus, the State party and the investor party *both* "must be taken to have consented to arbitration pursuant to the terms of Article 17(2)(a)."[187] According to the majority, because an investor would not be a party to the OIC Agreement, it could consent to arbitration only through its participation in the conciliation process outlined in Article 17(2)(a), and thus conciliation was a condition precedent to arbitration.[188]

183 *Itisaluna* (*supra* n 166) ¶ 160.
184 *Itisaluna* (*supra* n 166) ¶ 161.
185 *Itisaluna* (*supra* n 166) ¶ 187.
186 *Itisaluna* (*supra* n 166) ¶¶ 175–177.
187 *Itisaluna* (*supra* n 166) ¶ 189.
188 *Itisaluna* (*supra* n 166) ¶ 189.

The majority also held that the MFN clause under Article 8 of the OIC Agreement cannot be relied upon to import the host State's consent to ICSID arbitration from another investment treaty.[189] In this respect, the majority cited the well-known *Maffezini v. Spain* case which is the "jurisprudential font of the application of the MFN principle to dispute settlement rights".[190] The majority noted that the tribunal, in the *Maffezini* case, affirmed that the application of the MFN clause to dispute settlement mechanisms should be subject to "some important limits arising from public policy considerations" and it mentioned a number of situations for such restrictions.[191] Accordingly, in *Itisaluna*, the majority noted that three of these situations are present in the case at hand. In particular, the majority pointed out that the OIC Agreement "establishes a clearly defined and particular dispute settlement regime with institutional elements that include an arbitration forum with bespoke characteristics"; however, this Agreement does not refer to ICSID arbitration, "although it very easily could have done so".[192] Accordingly, the majority concluded that "this omission was a matter of conscious decision."[193] The majority also agreed with *Maffezini*'s statement that "a distinction has to be made between the legitimate extension of rights and benefits by means of the operation of the clause [MFN clause], on the one hand, and disruptive treaty-shopping that would play havoc with the policy objectives of underlying specific treaty provisions, on the other hand."[194]

The majority further observed that because the treaty makes no mention of ICSID arbitration specifically, it establishes consent to arbitrate only in *general terms*.[195] And, a "general consent to arbitrate does not constitute consent to ICSID arbitration, as required by Article 25(1) of the ICSID Convention."[196] Applying the Convention's self-evident requirement that consent to ICSID arbitration be "clear, specific and intended," the majority concluded that there was no clear basis in the OIC treaty to establish the parties' consent to ICSID arbitration, and for that reason jurisdiction *ratione voluntatis* must fail.[197]

189 *Itisaluna* (*supra* n 166) ¶ 223.
190 *Itisaluna* (*supra* n 166) ¶ 209.
191 *Itisaluna* (*supra* n 166) ¶¶ 210–211.
192 *Itisaluna* (*supra* n 166) ¶ 216.
193 *Itisaluna* (*supra* n 166) ¶ 216.
194 *Itisaluna* (*supra* n 166) ¶ 220.
195 *Itisaluna* (*supra* n 166) ¶¶ 190–191.
196 *Itisaluna* (*supra* n 166) ¶ 191.
197 *Itisaluna* (*supra* n 166) ¶ 221.

In light of the above, this award does seem to have foreclosed the access to the ICSID system under the auspices of the OIC Agreement, unless a future award adopted a different approach, or the parties agreed otherwise.

4.3.2 Dissenting Opinion

The dissenting opinion, meanwhile, found the claimant's arguments on the MFN clause sufficiently compelling to uphold ICSID jurisdiction over the case. According to the dissent, the majority's public policy concerns over excessive overreach were unsubstantiated, given that future arbitral tribunals would not be bound by the decision in *Itisaluna*.[198] Instead, the dissent argued that the interpretation of Article 17 of the UNCITRAL tribunal in *Al Warraq v. Indonesia*, i.e., that it "effectively creates an investor-[S]tate arbitration clause," was the correct one[199]

The dissent also agreed with *Al Warraq* tribunal's interpretation that, under Article 17, conciliation and arbitration are separate processes to be used either sequentially or alternatively.[200] The absence of prior conciliation between the parties, therefore, would not foreclose investor-State arbitration. The dissent further opined that Article 17's general consent to arbitration could be supplemented with the dispute resolution clause of the unrelated Iraq-Japan BIT to satisfy the Article 25(1) written consent requirement of the ICSID Convention.[201]

Finally, the dissent concluded that the MFN clause of the OIC Agreement applied to dispute settlement in the sense that such mechanisms are a "right or privilege accorded to investors" through the MFN clause.[202] While the dissent agreed with the majority that the OIC Agreement's MFN clause was "not a model of clarity,"[203] he believed that the lack of clarity empowered the Tribunal to decide the case at hand in accordance with the principles of treaty interpretation.

To date, *Itisaluna* is the only OIC arbitration initiated before an ICSID tribunal.[204]

198 *Itisaluna* (*supra* n 166) ¶ 229.
199 *Itisaluna* (*supra* n 166) ¶ 232.
200 *Itisaluna* (*supra* n 166) ¶ 234.
201 *Itisaluna* (*supra* n 166) ¶¶ 237–238.
202 *Itisaluna* (*supra* n 166) ¶ 235.
203 *Itisaluna* (*supra* n 166) ¶¶ 158, 214 and 241.
204 For a further detailed commentary on this case, see Mohamed S. Abdel Wahab, *Itisaluna and Others v Iraq: The OIC Agreement Conundrum: Consent to ICSID Arbitration and the MFN Clauses Saga*, ICSID Review, 1–13 (2020).

5 Substantive Protections

Once a tribunal establishes that it has jurisdiction over a claim, it will entertain the question of whether the host State has breached its substantive treaty obligations. Most investment treaties offer relatively similar types of substantive protections, although the scope of each substantive protection may vary.[205] The most essential protections found in the UAA and OIC treaties provide the right to: (i) full protection and security, (ii) free flow and transfer of capital, (iii) national treatment, (iv) most-favored-nation treatment, (v) fair and equitable treatment,[206] and (vi) compensation in the event of an expropriation. These protections will be discussed in further detail below.

5.1 *Full Protection and Security*

The notion of "protection and security" to be accorded to the investor appears in various forms in multilateral agreements. The classic framing in investment treaties is to provide "full protection and security."[207] A different, simpler iteration is to grant "protection" but not "security," whereas other formulations of the treaty rely on the "promise of 'legal security.'"[208] The tribunals interpreting these different formulations have read the protection to apply in different ways. Even in the absence of usage of "legal security," however, some tribunals have found that the "full protection and security" clause also provides protection against infringements of an investor's legal rights.[209] Other tribunals have taken the opposite view, limiting the scope of the protection to physical security.[210]

The notion of "protection and security" is unique in that it imposes positive obligations on the host State to protect investments, unlike the other standard

---

205 REDFERN (2015) (*supra* n 9) 8.78.

206 Only the amended version of the UAA provides the right to fair and equitable treatment. *See infra*, Section 5(5)(1).

207 RUDOLF DOLZER & CHRISTOPH SCHREUER, PRINCIPLES OF INTERNATIONAL INVESTMENT LAW (2012) 150.

208 DOLZER & SCHREUER (*supra* n 207) 150.

209 *See, e.g.*, *Azurix Corp. v. The Argentine Republic*, ICSID Case No. ARB/01/12, Award, 14 July 2006, ¶ 406 ("full protection and security may be breached even if no physical violence or damage occurs").

210 *See, e.g.*, *Rumeli Telekom A.S. and Telsim Mobil Telekomunikasyon Hizmetleri A.S. v. Republic of Kazakhstan*, ICSID Case No. ARB/05/16, Award, 29 July 2008, ¶ 668 ("The Arbitral Tribunal agrees with Respondent that the full protection and security standard ... obliges the State to provide a certain level of protection to foreign investment from physical damage").

substantive protections, which impose restrictions on host State action.[211] Breaches of the "full protection and security" obligation have been generally limited to situations in which the host State failed to prevent physical damage to investments by failing to exercise the governmental functions of policing and maintenance of law and order.[212] In *AAPL v. Sri Lanka*, the tribunal found that Sri Lanka breached the "full protection and security" obligation by not taking all possible measures to prevent a counterinsurgency operation that destroyed an investor's shrimp farm and killed several of its employees.[213]

The consensus, however, appears to be that even with the "full protection and security" language, "the standard does not provide absolute protection against physical or legal infringement."[214] It has been suggested that the host State is not operating under strict liability with an obligation to avoid all violations, but instead must demonstrate that it exercised "due diligence."[215] Tribunals will take into account the resources available to a State and the way in which the State employed those resources.[216] For example, a tribunal might find liability where, during a civil disturbance, the host State deployed its police only to locally owned establishments and did not extend similar protection to a foreign investor's factory. If, however, police resources had been deployed evenly,

211 Redfern (2015) (*supra* n 9) 8.113. *See also Parkerings-Compagniet AS v. Republic of Lithuania*, ICSID Case No. ARB/05/8, Award, 11 September 2007, ¶ 355 ("A violation of the standard of full protection and security could arise in case of failure of the State to prevent the damage, to restore the previous situation or to punish the author of the injury. The injury could be committed either by the host State, or by its agencies or by an individual.").

212 Redfern (2015) (*supra* n 9) 8.114 (citing *Asian Agricultural Products Ltd (AAPL) v. Republic of Sri Lanka*, ICSID Case No. ARB/87/3, Final Award, 27 June 1990, ¶ 86; *American Manufacturing and Trading Inc. v. Republic of Zaire*, ICSID Case No. ARB/93/1, Award, 21 February 1997, p. 41; *Rumeli Telekom AS and Telsim Mobil Telekomunikasyon Hizmetleri AS v. Republic of Kazakhstan*, Award, ICSID Case No. ARB/05/16, 29 July 2008, ¶ 668).

213 *Asian Agricultural Products Ltd (AAPL) v. Republic of Sri Lanka*, ICSID Case No. ARB/87/3, Final Award, 27 June 1990, ¶ 86.

214 Dolzer & Schreuer (*supra* n 207) 151.

215 Dolzer & Schreuer (*supra* n 207) 151; *Rumeli Telekom A.S. and Telsim Mobil Telekomunikasyon Hizmetleri A.S. v, Republic of Kazakhstan*, ICSID Case No. ARB/05/16, Award, 29 July 2008, ¶ 668 ("The Arbitral Tribunal agrees with Respondent that the full protection and security standard in Article II(2) of the UK-Kazakhstan BIT must be construed in accordance with the accepted rules of treaty interpretation. It obliges the State to provide a certain level of protection to foreign investment from physical damage. In *AMT v. Zaire* and in the *Wena* case, ICSID tribunals have recognized that in international law, the full protection and security obligation is one of 'due diligence' and no more.").

216 Redfern (2015) (*supra* n 9) 8.116.

and many businesses – domestic and foreign-owned alike – were damaged, a tribunal would likely not find liability.[217]

In cases of actions taken by the State itself, however, the "due diligence" requirement would not be implicated, and the State could be held "directly responsible."[218] At the same time, the standard is said not to be violated if the State action is pursuant to "its right to legislate and regulate and thereby takes reasonable measures under the circumstances."[219] As noted by the *Mamidoil v. Albania* tribunal:

> The Tribunal refers to a *jurisprudence constante* according to which the standard of constant protection and security does not imply strict liability but rather obliges States to use due diligence to prevent harassment and injuries to investors. The measure of due diligence is conditioned by the circumstances. The Tribunal further concurs with *Electrabel v. Hungary* that due diligence does not oblige the State to "prevent each and every injury".[220]

5.1.1 The Unified Arab Agreement

Article 2 of the General Provisions of the Unified Arab Agreement (as adopted in 1981) provides for the protection of the investments made by State Parties. Article 2 states that the State Parties to the Agreement "shall undertake" to protect the investor, his investment and the related revenues and rights "to the extent possible."[221] This provision uses the term "shall", but at the same time includes qualifying terms such as "undertake" and "to the extent possible" without providing objective and precise criteria therefor, which may allow the host States to deviate from this standard.[222]

Article 4, in contrast, provides that "[c]onclusions and interpretations derived from the provisions of this Agreement shall be guided by the principles on which it is based and the aims which inspired it, followed by the rules and principles common to the respective legislation of the States members of the League of Arab States and, finally, by the principles recognized in international

---

217 REDFERN (2015) (*supra* n 9) 8.116.
218 DOLZER & SCHREUER (*supra* n 207) 151.
219 DOLZER & SCHREUER (*supra* n 207) 151.
220 *Mamidoil Jetoil Greek Petroleum Products Societe Anonyme S.A. v. Republic of Albania*, ICSID Case No. ARB/11/24, Award, 30 March 2015, ¶ 821.
221 Unified Arab Agreement (*supra* n 1) Art. 2.
222 Abdel Wahab (*supra* n 51) 27 ¶ 38.

law."[223] Article 4 therefore suggests a hierarchy, by which the Agreement shall be interpreted in accordance with, first, "the principles on which it is based and the aims which inspired it," then, the rules and principles embedded in the domestic law of Member States, and last, principles of international law. The language of Article 2 might therefore be interpreted in the context of the Agreement's objectives, as well as established legal principles. It remains to be seen, however, how a tribunal might apply these interpretative principles to the treaty in practice.

In addition to the foregoing, Article 2 restricts the host State's obligation to promote and facilitate the investment to the investments which contribute to the economic development plans and programs of the host State.[224] However, Article 2 of the amended UAA of 2013 does not include such restriction, and it only mentions that the promotion and facilitation of the investment shall be "subject to the legislation and regulations concerning regulated activities and environmental protection.[225] Further, Article 2 of the amended UAA does not contain the above-mentioned words "to the extent possible".[226]

5.1.2 The OIC Agreement

Article 2 of the General Provisions of the OIC Agreement provides that the "contracting parties shall permit the transfer of capital among them and its utilization therein in the fields permitted for investment in accordance with their laws. The invested capital shall enjoy adequate protection and security and the host State shall give the necessary facilities and incentives to the investors engaged in activities therein."[227]

The standard of "*adequate* protection and security" may be read to fall short of the classical formulation of "*full* protection and security." This language could potentially be interpreted to provide greater leeway to the State, since in case of an adjudication between the State and an investor, the State need show only that "adequate" (not "full") protection and security was provided.

5.2 *Free Flow and Transfer of Capital*

Investors require freedom to transfer funds to host countries for investment purposes and, similarly, to repatriate returns to their home jurisdictions or to a third country. Therefore, the conditions for the transfer of funds into and out

223 Unified Arab Agreement (*supra* n 1) Art. 4. Similar wording used under Unified Arab Agreement as Amended in 2013 (supra n 60) Art. 4.

224 Abdel Wahab (*supra* n 51) 26–27 ¶ 37.

225 Unified Arab Agreement as Amended in 2013 (*supra* n 60) Art. 2.

226 Unified Arab Agreement as Amended in 2013 (supra n 60) Art. 2.

227 OIC Agreement (*supra* n 2) Art. 2.

of the host country are often a key concern of investors.[228] The host country, however, has a contrary concern related to the administration of its currency and foreign reserves.[229] Treaties, accordingly, do not typically grant an absolute right to transfer by investors. The right is usually restricted to certain types of transfers by inclusion of treaty language such as "transfers 'related to an investment,'"[230] and transfers "'subject to the laws' of the host State."[231]

5.2.1 The Unified Arab Agreement

In addition to providing the full protection and security clause, Article 2 provides that State Parties shall be permitted/allow "transfer Arab capital freely between them."[232] As mentioned above, Article 2 of the UAA (as adopted in 1981) includes a restriction to the scope of the protection and security standard and of the right to free transfer of the Arab capital to the investments contributing in the economic development of the host State.[233] However, Article 2 of the amended UAA of 2013 does not include such restriction.[234]

Article 7.1 of the UAA (as adopted in 1981) then elaborates that an "Arab investor shall have the freedom to make periodic transfers, both of Arab capital for investment in the territory … and of the revenues therefrom, and subsequently to make re-transfers to any State Party following settlement/fulfillment of his/her outstanding obligations without this being subject to any discriminatory banking, administrative or legal restrictions and without the transfer process incurring any taxes or duties. This shall not apply in respect of banking services."[235]

On a prima facie basis, this provision seems to establish the right to free transfer of the Arab capital. However, in fact, this provision further conditions this right on the settlement/fulfillment of the investor's outstanding obligations. As such, the investor is not entitled to re-transfer the investment's capital and revenues unless it had, first, settled/fufilled its outstanding obligations.

---

228 DOLZER & SCHREUER (*supra* n 207) 180.
229 DOLZER & SCHREUER (*supra* n 207) 181.
230 DOLZER & SCHREUER (*supra* n 207) 181.
231 DOLZER & SCHREUER (*supra* n 207) 181.
232 Unified Arab Agreement (*supra* n 1) Art. 2 using the words 'shall be permitted'; *see also* Unified Arab Agreement as Amended in 2013 (*supra* n 60) Art. 2 using the words 'shall allow'.
233 Abdel Wahab (*supra* n 51) 32 ¶ 56.
234 Unified Arab Agreement as Amended in 2013 (*supra* n 60) Art. 2.
235 Unified Arab Agreement (*supra* n 1) Art. 7.1; *see also* Unified Arab Agreement as Amended in 2013 (*supra* n 60) Art. 6.1.

Nonetheless, this provision does not set out the nature of such obligations.[236] More specifically, this provision does not clarify whether such investor's obligations are intended to be its obligations towards the host State or towards other investors in the territory of the host State. Moreover, this provision does not identify the source of such obligation, i.e. whether its source is the investment itself in question, is related thereto or does not need to be related to this investment. For instance, it is not clear whether the Arab investor may be prevented from re-transferring its capital in the case where a creditor from a third State, which is not a party to the UAA, initiated enforcement proceedings against the proprieties/assets of this Arab investor.[237]

In this context, the UAA amendment of 2013 introduced a further clarification regarding the obligations precluding the re-transfer of the Arab capital and revenues. Article 6.1 of the amended UAA states that:

> The Arab investor shall be free to … subsequently re-transfer the same to any State Party without delay following settlement [fulfillement] of his/her outstanding legal obligations arising from the investment project and owed to the host State …[238]

Further to the above restriction under the UAA (as adopted in 1981), Article 7.2 does not allow the Arab investor to re-transfer the original capital before the termination of the investment according to its nature or before a period of five years from the date of its transfer, whichever is shorter.[239] In our view, such time limit is not common in investment agreements and is not justified. That explains why this provision does not feature in the UAA amendment of 2013.

5.2.2 The OIC Agreement

Article 2 of the OIC Agreement permits the contracting parties to transfer capital and utilize it in the fields permitted for investment; however, the right to the free transfer of capital is embedded in Article 11.[240] Article 11.1 of the OIC Agreement provides that the "host State shall undertake to guarantee the free transfer to any contracting party of the capitals and its net proceeds in cash

236 Abdel Wahab (*supra* n 51) 31 ¶ 52.
237 Abdel Wahab (*supra* n 51) 31 ¶ 52.
238 Unified Arab Agreement as Amended in 2013 (*supra* n 60) Art. 6.1.
239 Unified Arab Agreement (*supra* n 1) Art. 7.2.
240 OIC Agreement (*supra* n 2) Art. 2 ("The contracting parties shall permit the transfer of capitals among them and its utilization therein in the fields permitted for investment in accordance with their laws").

without the investor being subject to any discriminatory banking, administrative or legal restrictions and without any taxes or charges on the transfer. This shall not apply to the bank service charges."[241]

Article 11.1 further states that "the repatriation of the original capital shall be effected on the termination of the investment according to its nature or after five years from the date of its transfer to the host state, whichever is earlier". Accordingly, unlike the UAA, the OIC Agreement does not condition the re-transfer of the capital or revenues on the settlement of the investors' obligations. However, like the UAA adopted in 1981 (but unlike the amended UAA of 2013), the OIC Agreement sets out a time limit for the repatriation of the original capital.

5.3 *National Treatment Clause*

A national treatment clause requires "non-discrimination between similarly situated domestic and foreign persons, entities, goods, services or investments."[242] This clause provides a relative standard of protection, and, thus, its scope cannot be articulated in absolute terms, but rather will vary according to the circumstances of each case.[243] Therefore, tribunals applying a national treatment clause will evaluate whether the host State provided the same level of treatment to both domestic and foreign investors.[244]

There are three steps of analysis that are required before a determination is made that the national treatment standard has been violated.[245] First, the investor must identify an existing comparator – i.e., a similarly situated domestic investor.[246] Second, a tribunal must determine whether the treatment accorded to the foreign investor is not as favorable than the treatment accorded to the domestic comparator.[247] Third, if the treatment of the foreign investor is less favorable, it has to be determined whether that difference in treatment is justified.[248] Even though not usually spelled out in the agreements, differences

241 OIC Agreement (*supra* n 2) Art 11.

242 ANDREW NEWCOMBE & LLUÍS PARADELL, LAW AND PRACTICE OF INVESTMENT TREATIES: STANDARDS OF TREATMENT (2009) 147.

243 REDFERN (2015) (*supra* n 9) 8.125.

244 REDFERN (2015) (*supra* n 9) 8.125.

245 DOLZER & SCHREUER (*supra* n 207) 172.

246 DOLZER & SCHREUER (*supra* n 207) 172; *United Parcel Service of America Inc. v Government of Canada*, Award, UNCITRAL, 24 May 2007, ¶¶ 173–184.

247 DOLZER & SCHREUER (*supra* n 207) 172; *United Parcel Service of America Inc. v Government of Canada*, Award, UNCITRAL, 24 May 2007, ¶¶ 173–184.

248 DOLZER & SCHREUER (*supra* n 207) 172.

in treatment can, at times, be considered justifiable if legitimate policy objectives are shown.[249]

5.3.1 The Unified Arab Agreement

Article 6 includes the national treatment provision in providing that:

> In accordance with the provision of the preceding article, in the State Party where the investment is made, the capital of the Arab investor shall, without discrimination, be treated in the same manner as capital owned by the citizens of that State. It shall automatically acquire identical legal status in terms of rights, obligations, regulations and procedures, although this shall not apply to any additional concessions, which the State Party may accord to an Arab investment.[250]

This clause establishes protection from discrimination against foreign capital. The terms "without discrimination" and "identical legal status" ensure that Arab foreign investors receive the same treatment as domestic investors, and this guarantee is not qualified.

5.3.2 The OIC Agreement

Article 14 of the OIC Agreement provides that:

> The investor shall be accorded a treatment not less than that accorded by the host State to its national investors or others regarding the compensation of damage that may befall the physical assets of investment due to hostilities of international nature committed by any international body or due to civil disturbances or violent acts of general nature.

Even though Article 14 requires the host State to accord the same treatment to investors from other member States as it would its own nationals, the provision is limited in application to situations where compensation is owed "due to hostilities of international nature committed by any international body or due to civil disturbances or violent acts of general nature."[251] Therefore, the scope of

249 Dolzer & Schreuer (*supra* n 207) 174; *Gami Investments Inc. v. The Government of the United Mexican States*, Award, UNCITRAL, 15 November 2004, ¶ 114.

250 Unified Arab Agreement (*supra* n 1) Art. 6; *see also* Unified Arab Agreement as Amended in 2013 (*supra* n 60) Art. 5.2 ("In the host State, invested Arab capital shall be treated in a manner not less favourable than the capital owned by the citizens of said State or a third State, whichever is more favourable and without discrimination.").

251 OIC Agreement (*supra* n 2) Art. 14.

national treatment protection provided by the OIC Agreement appears to be more limited than that in the Unified Arab Agreement.

5.4 *Most-Favored Nation*

As introduced above, the MFN obligation requires that the State does not "discriminate between similarly situated foreign persons, entities, goods, services or investments."[252] MFN treatment seeks to put the investor in a position where it is accorded "equality of opportunity on the highest possible plane," since with the MFN clause the investor has a right to the "maximum of favors conceded to any third State."[253] Through an MFN clause, a State can "obtain the benefits and advantages that more powerful States might be able to obtain in treaty negotiations."[254] There is disagreement over whether the MFN clause applies in the abstract, where an investor can identify a third treaty that provides superior protections, but cannot identify an existing investor that has received those same protections. Such a concrete comparator might be required where the MFN clause requires the host State to treat investors in a manner no less favorable than how they treat investors for third States "in similar circumstances."[255]

Traditionally, investors have relied on the MFN clause to import substantive rights from third treaties.[256] For example, if the host State provides tax concessions to Spanish investors in the electronics industry, but not to Chinese investors in that same industry, a Chinese investor could rely on an MFN clause to claim compensation for the loss suffered as a result of the discrimination.[257] More recently – and as illustrated by the debate in the *Itisaluna* case discussed above – some tribunals have extended the application of MFN protection to procedural matters, such as the dispute resolution mechanism between the host State and investors.[258] For example, in *Maffezini v. Spain*, the tribunal allowed the investor to rely on the more favorable arrangement contained in a third BIT that permitted an investor to submit its dispute to ICSID arbitration

252 Newcombe & Paradell (*supra* n 242) 193.

253 Newcombe & Paradell (*supra* n 242) 195.

254 Newcombe & Paradell (*supra* n 242) 195.

255 *See, e.g.*, *İçkale İnşaat Limited Şirketi v. Turkmenistán*, ICSID Case No. ARB/10/24, Award, 8 March 2016, ¶ 329; *Apotex Holdings Inc. and Apotex Inc. v. United States of America*, ICSID Case No ARB(AF)/12/1, Award, 25 December 2014, ¶¶ 8.15–8.17.

256 Redfern (2015) (*supra* n 9) 8.127.

257 Redfern (2015) (*supra* n 9) 8.127.

258 *See, e.g.*, *EDF International and others v. Argentine Republic*, ICSID Case No. ARB/03/23, Award, 11 June 2012, ¶ 929.

without first accessing the local courts.[259] In other cases – for example, *Plama v. Bulgaria* – tribunals have maintained the traditional view that MFN clauses do not extend to procedural rights.[260] In this respect, the *Palma* tribunal affirmed that "the intention to incorporate dispute settlement provisions must be 'clearly and unambiguously expressed" and that the principle with multiple exceptions as stated by the tribunal in the Maffezini case should instead be a different principle with one single exception: an MFN provision in a basic treaty does not incorporate by reference dispute settlement provisions in whole or in part set forth in another treaty, unless the MFN provision in the basic treaty leaves no doubt that the Contracting Parties intended to incorporate them."[261]

This inconsistent jurisprudence has led to a new generation of investment treaties that expressly exclude procedural rights from the scope of the MFN clause.[262] These issues surrounding the scope of an MFN clause remain controversial in investor-state arbitration.

5.4.1 The Unified Arab Agreement

The Unified Arab Agreement (as adopted in 1981) seems to not include an MFN clause of the nature one would expect to see in investment treaties. The provision which may be argued to be close to an MFN clause, is Article 6.2 which reads:

> An Arab Investor may opt for any other treatment accorded to a non-Arab investment in a similar field in the State where the investment takes place pursuant to a legislation or an international agreement. This shall not apply to any distinct treatment granted for a specific project due to its special importance to such State.[263]

---

259 *Emilio Agustín Maffezini v. The Kingdom of Spain*, ICSID Case No. ARB/97/7, Decision of the Tribunal on Objections to Jurisdiction, 25 January 2000, ¶ 64.

260 *Plama Consortium Limited v. Republic of Bulgaria*, ICSID Case No. ARB/03/24, Decision on Jurisdiction, 8 February 2005, ¶ 223 ("an MFN provision in a basic treaty does not incorporate by reference dispute settlement provisions in whole or in part set forth in another treaty, unless the MFN provision in the basic treaty leaves no doubt that the Contracting Parties intended to incorporate them").

261 *Plama* (*supra* n 260) ¶ 204 and 223.

262 REDFERN (2015) (*supra* n 9) 8. 127. *See also*, UNCTAD, *Most-Favored-Nation Treatment: A Sequel*, SERIES ON ISSUES IN INTERNATIONAL INVESTMENT AGREEMENTS No. II (2010), http://unctad.org/en/Docs/diaeia20101_en.pdf, pp. 85–86 (referring to the Chile–Colombia FTA of 2006, Annex 9.3, the Canada–Peru FTA of 2008, Annex 804.1, and the Japan–Switzerland EPA of 2009, Art. 88).

263 Unified Arab Agreement (*supra* n 1) Art. 6.2; *see also* Unified Arab Agreement as Amended in 2013 (*supra* n 60) Art. 5.3.

This provision does not, automatically, grant the investor the right to benefit from the privileges conferred on non-Arab investors.[264] Quite interestingly, this provision expressly allows the host State to treat an investment more favorably than another investment in light of "its special importance to such State" without providing any objective or precise criteria for such importance.[265]

However, the UAA amendment of 2013 introduced a clear MFN clause under its Article 5.2:[266]

> In the host State, invested Arab capital shall be treated in a manner not less favourable than the capital owned by the citizens of the said State or a third State, whichever is more favourable and without discrimination.[267]

Comparing the wording of Articles 6.2 of the 1981 UAA and 5.2 of the 2013 UAA shows that the former does not qualify as an MFN clause. This is also supported by the fact that when an MFN provision was added in the 2013 amendment of the UAA, Article 6.2 was neither deleted nor significantly amended. Article 6.2 of the 1981 UAA was retained with minor amendments while Article 5.2 providing for an MFN clause was added by virtue of the 2013 amendment.[268]

In addition to the above, Article 9.2 of the amended UAA requires the host States to grant the Arab investor a treatment not less favorable than that granted to the investors of that State or of a third State in case of incurring a loss resulting from a war or a national emergency in this host State.[269]

Notwithstanding the foregoing, similar to the approach followed in some bilateral investment treaties ("BITs"), the amended UAA sets out under

264 Abdel Wahab (*supra* n 51) 36 ¶ 69.

265 Abdel Wahab (*supra* n 51) 36 ¶ 69.

266 Hamida (2013) (*supra* n 78) 7; Nassib G. Ziadé, *Arbitration under MENA Regional Investment Treaties*, in Arbitration: The International Journal of Arbitration, Mediation and Dispute Management (O'Reilly (ed.), Chartered Institute of Arbitrators (CIArb), (2017) 50.

267 Unified Arab Agreement as Amended in 2013 (*supra* n 60) Art. 5.2.

268 Unified Arab Agreement as Amended in 2013 (*supra* n 60) Art. 5.3 which provides that: "The Arab investor shall be entitled to opt for any other manner of treatment which is laid down in general provisions in force in the host State under any law, international agreement or other investment agreements. This shall not include any privileged treatment accorded by the State in respect of a specific investment which due to its particular importance to that State."

269 Unified Arab Agreement as Amended in 2013 (*supra* n 60) Art. 9.2.

Article 5.4 a list of exceptional privileges which are not subject to the protections of national treatment and MFN as follows:[270]

> The provisions of this Article shall not apply to the following:
> (a) The privileges granted by any contact party to the investors of a third state pursuant to its membership of a free trade area, customs union or common market.
> (b) Tax or zakat treatment.
> (c) Ownership of land and real estate.

In addition to the above, like the 1981 UAA, the amended UAA of 2013 allows the host State to treat an investment more favorably than another investment due to the special/particular importance of this investment to the host State.[271] Further, the UAA expressly allows host States to grant Arab investors a favorable/preferential treatment.[272] Such power of providing a favorable/preferential treatment may be subject to abuse, particularly in the absence of clear and precise criteria for the grant of such preferential treatment.

5.4.2 The OIC Agreement

Article 8 contains the OIC Agreement's MFN provision. Article 8 provides that:

1. The investors of any contracting party shall enjoy, within the context of economic activity in which they have employed their investments in the territories of another contracting party, a treatment not less favourable than the treatment accorded to investors belonging to another State not party to this Agreement, in the context of that activity and in respect of rights and privileges accorded to those investors.
2. Provisions of paragraph 1 above shall not be applied to any better treatment given by a contracting party in the following cases:
    a. Rights and privileges given to investors of one contracting party by another contracting party in accordance with an international agreement, law or special preferential arrangement.
    b. Rights and privileges arising from an international agreement currently in force or to be concluded in the future and to which any contracting party may become a member and under which an

270 Unified Arab Agreement as Amended in 2013 (*supra* n 60) Art. 5.4; Abdel Wahab (*supra* n 51) 37 ¶ 71.

271 Unified Arab Agreement (*supra* n 1) Art. 6.2; Unified Arab Agreement as Amended in 2013 (*supra* n 60) Art. 5.3.

272 Unified Arab Agreement (*supra* n 1) Art. 16; Unified Arab Agreement as Amended in 2013 (*supra* n 60) Art. 14.

economic union, customs union or mutual tax exemption arrangement is set up.

c. Rights and privileges given by a contracting party for a specific project due to its special importance to that State.

Article 8(1) ensures that investors will not be treated less favorably than investors from noncontracting parties when engaged in the same sphere of economic activity. This guarantee is not without limit, as Article 8(2) imposes limitations on the application of the MFN provision.[273]

As discussed, *supra*, the tribunal in *Itisaluna et al. v. Iraq*, analyzed whether the claimants could rely on the MFN provision of the OIC Agreement to import an ICSID arbitration clause found in the Iraq-Japan bilateral investment treaty. The majority ultimately rejected this interpretation because it would invariably allow an unrelated bilateral investment treaty to change the meaning of the OIC Agreement and compromise its multilateral character.[274] Moreover, the majority identified an express limitation on the application of the MFN clause in Article 8(2)(a), which provides that it shall not apply to any better treatment given by a Contracting Party in the case of "[r]ights and privileges given to investors of one contracting party by another contracting party in accordance with an international agreement, law or special preferential arrangement." In effect, the majority ruled that the MFN clause of the OIC Agreement could not be relied upon as a great "leveler" of rights and privileges to "circumvent such differential treatment."[275]

5.5 *Fair and Equitable Treatment* (FET)

The vast majority of investment treaties currently in force require the host State to provide foreign investors with fair and equitable treatment ("FET"), which is the standard most commonly invoked in investment arbitrations.[276]

273 OIC Agreement (*supra* n 2) Art. 8.2.

274 *Itisaluna* (*supra* n 166) ¶¶ 190–191.

275 *Itisaluna* (*supra* n 166) ¶¶ 198–199.

276 UNCTAD, *Fair and Equitable Treatment: A Sequel*, SERIES ON ISSUES IN INTERNATIONAL INVESTMENT AGREEMENTS No. II (2012), 17–35, http://unctad.org/en/Docs/unctaddiaeia2011d5_en.pdf, (identifying the five "most important and widespread approaches to the FET standard in treaty practice … (a) Prohibition of manifest arbitrariness in decision-making, that is, measures taken purely on the basis of prejudice or bias without a legitimate purpose or rational explanation; (b) Prohibition of the denial of justice and disregard of the fundamental principles of due process; (c) Prohibition of targeted discrimination on manifestly wrongful grounds, such as gender, race or religious belief; (d) Prohibition of abusive treatment of investors, including coercion, duress and harassment; (e) Protection of the legitimate expectations of investors arising from a

The FET standard is not determined by the laws of the host State, but is rather meant as a rule of international law.[277]

The text of FET clauses varies among different treaties.[278] FET clauses typically refer to a vague standard of "fair and equitable treatment," without further descriptive language to define the standard's requirements. Some treaties expressly refer to a "minimum standard of treatment" in accordance with international law; others refer only to international law, without reference to a minimum standard; a third category of treaties sets forth the FET obligation without any reference to international law at all.[279]

Tribunals disagree over whether the term "fair and equitable treatment" is synonymous with the minimum standard of protection required by customary international law, or whether FET requires greater protection.[280] Under customary international law, the minimum standard has traditionally been understood as set forth in the *Neer v. Mexico* case:

> [T]he treatment of an alien, in order to constitute an international delinquency, should amount to an outrage, to bad faith, to wilful neglect of duty, or to an insufficiency of governmental action so far short of international standards that every reasonable and impartial man would readily recognize its insufficiency.[281]

Some tribunals have found that the minimum standard of protection has evolved substantially since *Neer* was decided, such that the term is now indistinguishable from FET.[282] For example, the NAFTA tribunal in *Mondev v. United States* applied the customary international law standard and observed:

> To the modern eye, what is unfair or inequitable need not equate with the outrageous or the egregious. In particular, a State may treat foreign

government's specific representations or investmentinducing [sic] measures, although balanced with the host State's right to regulate in the public interest").

277 DOLZER & SCHREUER (*supra* n 207) 131.

278 Jean Kalicki, *Fair, Equitable and Ambiguous*, 22 ICSID REV. FILJ 24, 26–27 (2007).

279 Jean Kalicki, (*supra* n 278) 27 (2007).

280 REDFERN (2015) (*supra* n 9) ¶ 8.106; *BG Group PLC v. Republic of Argentina*, Final Award, UNCITRAL, 24 December 2007, ¶¶ 275–310.

281 Redfern (2015) (*supra* n 9) ¶ 8.106; *Neer v. Mexico*, Opinion, United States–Mexico General Claims Commission, 4 RIAA 60, 15 October 1926, ¶¶ 61–62.

282 *See, e.g., Pope & Talbot Inc. v. Government of Canada*, Award on Damages, UNCITRAL, 31 May 2002, ¶¶ 52, 55; *International Thunderbird Gaming Corporation v. The United Mexican States*, UNCITRAL ad hoc, Award, 26 January 2006, ¶ 194.

> investment unfairly and inequitably without necessarily acting in bad faith.[283]

The precise scope of the FET clause often depends on the language used and the views of a particular tribunal deciding the issue. The FET standard is, generally, determined and interpreted on a case-by-case basis. Notwithstanding the foregoing, the FET standard requires, in any event, the host State to provide a transparent and stable economic environment, to respect the investor's legitimate expectations and to establish legal security.[284]

5.5.1 The Unified Arab Agreement

There is no FET provision in the original Unified Arab Agreement. However, as noted above, the amended version of the UAA does contain an FET provision under its Article 2. That provision states that "Arab capital in the State Party shall benefit from fair and equitable treatment at all times [.]"[285] Nonetheless, this FET standard seems to be "general and unqualified, affording tribunals broad discretion in determining what constitutes a breach of the standard."[286]

5.5.2 The OIC Agreement

Although the OIC Agreement also contains no FET provision, some tribunals have permitted investors to rely on the MFN provision to import an FET provision from another agreement to which the host country belongs.[287] For example, in *Al-Warraq*, the claimant sought to import the FET obligation in Article 3 of the UK-Indonesia BIT by virtue of the MFN clause in Article 8 of the OIC Agreement.[288]

The tribunal in *Al-Warraq* considered the UK-Indonesia BIT by analyzing the text of the two treaties and identifying a similar purpose.[289] The tribunal also considered various other BITs, including the Netherlands-Indonesia BIT, Singapore-Indonesia BIT and the India-Indonesia BIT, where Indonesia agreed to accord fair and equitable treatment to foreign investors, and concluded that *Al-Warraq* was entitled to fair and equitable treatment protection through the

283 *Mondev International Ltd v. United States of America*, ICSID Case No. ARB(AF)/99/2, Final Award, 11 October 2002, ¶ 116.
284 Abdel Wahab (*supra* n 51) 25–26 ¶ 31 and 33.
285 Unified Arab Agreement as Amended in 2013 (*supra* n 60) Art. 2.
286 Mouawad & Khoury (*supra* n 36), 249–250.
287 *Al-Warraq* (*supra* n 160) ¶ 541.
288 *Al-Warraq* (*supra* n 160) ¶ 540.
289 *Al-Warraq* (*supra* n 160) ¶¶ 549–51 (comparing preambles of UK-Indonesia BIT and the OIC Agreement).

OIC Agreement's MFN Clause.[290] According to the tribunal, "the MFN clause [of the OIC Agreement] applies to import other clauses as long as the *ejusdem generis* rule applies."[291] In other words, the MFN clause may import an FET provision so long as the two agreements represent the same subject matter.[292] After analyzing the preambles of each of the treaties, the tribunal observed that the subject matter – the protection of foreign investments – was the same in both treaties.[293] The tribunal concluded that Indonesia had breached its obligations under the OIC Agreement because its unfair criminal prosecution of an investor had violated the FET provision from another BIT.[294] However, the tribunal held that the investor's claim for damages based on the breach of the FET is inadmissible on the basis of the "clean hands" doctrine due to the investor's wrongdoings in relation to bank activities.[295]

5.6 *Expropriation*

Expropriation protection in the investor agreements ensures that the State does not "openly and deliberately seize[]" property from the investors for itself or a third party.[296] The protection extends to situations where a State adopts measures that deprive the investor of its property or its benefit.[297] This protection, however, is not absolute. A State, for instance, does not incur responsibility for the "legitimate and bonafide exercise of sovereign police powers subject to specific commitments or an analysis for proportionality and reasonableness."[298]

The obligation to compensate for expropriation is "among the most crucial protections provided by investment treaties,"[299] and expropriation provisions are frequently relied upon by investors.[300] A typical provision establishes that

290 *Al-Warraq* (*supra* n 160) ¶¶ 554–555.

291 *Al-Warraq* (*supra* n 160) ¶ 551.

292 *Al-Warraq* (*supra* n 160); *see also* OECD, *Most-Favoured-Nation Treatment in International Investment Law*, OECD Working Papers on International Investment (2004), http://dx.doi.org/10.1787/518757021651 (explaining that "t[]he *ejusdem generis* principle is the rule according to which a MFN clause can only attract matters belonging to the same subject matter or the same category of subject as to which the clause relates").

293 *Al-Warraq* (*supra* n 160) ¶ 551.

294 Mouawad & Khoury (*supra* n 36) 256. Despite finding the breach of the FET provision, the Tribunal nonetheless prohibited the investor from pursuing the claim due to conduct in violation of the equitable principle of unclean hands. Mouawad & Khoury (*supra* n 36) 256.

295 *Al-Warraq* (*supra* n 160) ¶ 646.

296 Newcombe & Paradell (*supra* n 242) 321.

297 Newcombe & Paradell (*supra* n 242) 321.

298 Newcombe & Paradell (*supra* n 242) 321.

299 REDFERN (2015) (*supra* n 9) ¶ 8.79.

300 REDFERN (2015) (*supra* n 9) ¶ 8.79.

for an expropriation to be legal, it must be (i) for a public purpose, (ii) nondiscriminatory, (iii) in accordance with due process, and (iv) upon payment of prompt, adequate, and effective compensation.[301]

Investment treaties protect against both direct and indirect expropriations that do not satisfy the above criteria. A direct expropriation occurs when a host State effects an outright seizure of a foreign investor's property or title. In such cases, "there is an open, deliberate and unequivocal intent, as reflected in a formal law or decree or physical act, to deprive the owner of his or her property through the transfer of title or outright seizure."[302] For example, in *Funnekotter v. Zimbabwe*, the tribunal found that Zimbabwe had expropriated the claimants' investments in commercial farms when it physically took the farms pursuant to a government land acquisition program.[303]

Expropriation may also occur indirectly. This takes place when a State enacts measures that result in deprivation of the use and value of the investment, even though the actual title of the asset remains with the investor.[304] As explained in *Ronald S. Lauder v. The Czech Republic*: "The concept of indirect (or 'de facto', or 'creeping') expropriation is not clearly defined. Indirect expropriation or nationalization is a measure that does not involve an overt taking, but that effectively neutralizes the enjoyment of the property."[305] International arbitral tribunals have relied on this principle to award damages for indirect expropriation where a host State has not seized an investment, but has taken measures that have destroyed its value.[306] A "creeping" expropriation is a form of indirect expropriation that results from a series of measures over time that taken individually do not amount to expropriation, but that in the aggregate have an expropriatory effect.

---

301 REDFERN (2015) (*supra* n 9) ¶ 8.80.

302 UNCTAD, *Expropriation: A Sequel*, SERIES ON ISSUES IN INTERNATIONAL INVESTMENT AGREEMENTS No. II, p.7 (2012), http://unctad.org/en/Docs/unctaddiaeia2011d7_en.pdf.

303 *Bernardus Henricus Funnekotter and others v. Republic of Zimbabwe*, ICSID Case No. ARB/05/6, Award, 22 April 2009, ¶ 148.

304 OECD, *Indirect Expropriation and the Right to Regulate in International Investment Law*, Working Paper on International Investment No. 2004/4 (2004), http://www.oecd.org/daf/inv/investment-policy/WP-2004_4.pdf.

305 *Ronald S. Lauder v. Czech Republic*, UNCITRAL ad hoc, Final Award, 3 September 2001, ¶ 200.

306 REDFERN (2015) (*supra* n 9) ¶ 8.83. *See, e.g., Total S.A. v. the Argentine Republic*, ICSID Case No. ARB/04/01, Award, 27 December 2010, ¶ 195 ("[U]nder international law a measure which does not have all the features of a formal expropriation could be equivalent to an expropriation if an effective deprivation of the investment is thereby caused. An effective deprivation requires, however, a total loss of value of the property such as when the property affected is rendered worthless by the measure, as in case of direct expropriation, even if formal title continues to be held").

5.6.1 The Unified Arab Agreement

Article 9 of the Unified Arab Agreement includes a detailed expropriation clause:

1. According to the provisions of this Agreement, the capital of the Arab investor shall not be subject to any specific or general measures, whether permanent or temporary and irrespective of their legal form, which wholly or partially affect any of the assets, reserves or revenues of the investor and which lead to confiscation, compulsory seizure, dispossession, nationalization, liquidation, dissolution, the extortion or elimination of secrets regarding technical ownership or other material rights, the forcible prevention or delay of debt settlement or any other measures leading to the sequestration, freezing or administration of assets, or any other action which infringes the right of ownership itself or prejudices the intrinsic authority of the owner in terms of his control and possession of the investment, his right to administer it, his acquisition of the revenues therefrom or the fulfilment of his rights and the discharge of his obligations.
2. It shall, however, be permissible to:
   a. Seize property for the public benefit in accordance with the authority vested in the State or its institutions to perform their functions in implementing public projects, provided that this is done on a non-discriminatory basis in return for fair compensation and according to general legal provisions regulating the seizure of property for the purposes of the public benefit. The Arab investor shall be given the opportunity to challenge the legitimacy of any dispossession and the amount of compensation before the domestic courts. Compensation shall be made within a period not exceeding one year from the date when the decision to dispossess became final;
   b. Take precautionary measures at the order of a competent judicial authority and measures to implement judgements delivered by a competent judicial authority.[307]

The wording of Article 9.1 shows that the UAA adopts the same definition of expropriation enshrined in the majority of the BITs by protecting the investor from both direct or indirect expropriation. Moreover, Article 9.2 provides the usual reservation that a State may "seize property for the public benefit" so long as the seizure is "done on a non-discriminatory basis," and "fair compensation"

307 Unified Arab Agreement (*supra* n 1) Art. 9; *see also* Unified Arab Agreement as Amended in 2013 (*supra* n 60) Art. 8.

is provided and is in accordance with "general legal provisions regulating the seizure of property for the purposes of the public benefit."

In this respect, the amended UAA provides further clarification in relation to the compensation due in the case of expropriation. Article 8.2(a) of the amended UAA states that the fair compensation in the case of expropriation is "equal to the market value of the investment before making the expropriation decision to seize the property or it being made known to the public, whichever comes first. If it is not possible to verify the market value, compensation shall be set in accordance with generally recognised principles for assessment and on the basis of equitable principles that take into consideration, inter alia, the investor's capital, depreciation, cost of replacement and other relevant factors."[308]

This provision also grants the investor a right to interest in case of delay in the payment of the said compensation by the host State.[309]

5.6.2 The OIC Agreement

Article 10.1 of the OIC Agreement protects the investor generally from direct and indirect expropriation. Article 10 provides:

1. The host State shall undertake not to adopt or permit the adoption of any measure – itself or through one of its organs, institutions or local authorities – if such a measure may directly or indirectly affect the ownership of the investor's capital or investment by depriving him totally or partially of his ownership or of all or part of his basic rights or the exercise of his authority on the ownership, possession or utilization of his capital, or of his actual control over the investment, its management, making use out of it, enjoying its utilities, the realization of its benefits or guaranteeing its development and growth.
2. It will, however, be permissible to: (a) Expropriate the investment in the public interest in accordance with the law, without discrimination and on prompt payment of adequate and effective compensation to the investor in accordance with the laws of the host State regulating such compensation, provided that the investor shall have the right to contest the measure of expropriation in the competent court of the host State. (b) Adopt preventive measures issued in accordance with an order from a competent legal authority and the execution measures of the decision given by a competent judicial authority."[310]

308 Unified Arab Agreement as Amended in 2013 (*supra* n 60) Art. 8.2(a).
309 Unified Arab Agreement as Amended in 2013 (*supra* n 60) Art. 8.2(a).
310 OIC Agreement (*supra* n 2) Art. 10.

The language of this provision appears "relatively broad,"[311] setting forth a range of scenarios in which a State measure might constitute an expropriation. In practice, however, Article 10.1 describes the range of action that is commonly understood to comprise the standard of expropriation in international investment law. In that regard, Article 10.2 carves out the typical exceptions, allowing for expropriations that are "in the public interest," non-discriminatory, and "on prompt payment of adequate and effective compensation."

5.7 *Comparison of the Standards of Protection Found in the Agreements*

Broadly speaking, the Unified Arab Agreement as adopted in 1981 and the OIC Agreement provide comparable protections. However, when these agreements are compared with the UAA amendment of 2013, the latter seems to be providing, in some areas, more expansive investment protection.

For instance, the 1981 UAA requires host States to provide the protection and security to the investors to "the extent possible" and it restricts this standard to the investments contributing to the economic development of the State. In relation to the same standard, the OIC Agreement's Article 2 requires the host State to provide an "adequate protection" and not a 'full' protection, but without including the aforementioned economic-related restriction. Less restrictively, the amended UAA makes no mention of the words "to the extent possible" and excludes the restriction related to economic development.

The UAA further provides that host countries shall, to the extent possible, ensure the stability of pertinent legal provisions. Such a requirement is not present in the OIC Agreement.[312] Moreover, the OIC Agreement mentions only once – in the preamble – that its provisions are a "minimum" for the treatment of capital and investments within OIC Member States. In contrast, the UAA employs the "minimum standard" language not only in the preamble, but also in Article 3, which explicitly notes that the provisions of the Agreement "shall constitute a minimum standard to be applied in the treatment of any investment subject thereto."[313] The inclusion of this language in the main body of the UAA could help to bolster protections for investors.

Further, the national treatment provision of the OIC Agreement seems significantly limited when compared with the national treatment provision in the UAA. Article 14 of the OIC Agreement restricts the application of national treatment to the compensation for the damages resulting from circumstances involving international hostilities, civil disturbances, or violent acts. The UAA

---

311 Rosher (*supra* n 161).
312 Unified Arab Agreement (*supra* n 1) Art. 2.
313 Unified Arab Agreement (*supra* n 1) Art. 3.

does include a national treatment provision without containing any such restrictions.

Finally, the OIC Agreement provides no FET provision. Nonetheless, it is possible that the absence of the FET provision in the OIC Agreement may lose significance, since the tribunal in *Al-Warraq* has set a precedent for importing FET provisions via the MFN provision.[314] It remains to be seen, though, whether other tribunals will follow the *Al-Warraq* approach. Similarly, the 1981 UAA does not include an FET provision. In comparison, the UAA amendment of 2013 to the UAA explicitly includes an FET clause which may be relied upon by the Arab investors against the States that have ratified this amendment.

There are some more limited ways in which the OIC Agreement appears to provide greater protection to investors than does the UAA. First, the expropriation standard in the OIC Agreement requires prompt, adequate, and effective compensation.[315] By contrast, the UAA requires only that compensation be "fair," which is arguably a vaguer standard.[316] However, the amended UAA links the fair compensation to the market value of the investment before the expropriation decision.

Second, in the UAA, the investor's right to free transfer of capital is subject to several restrictions as discussed above. Notably, the investor is only entitled to re-transfer of the capital and revenues upon settlement/fulfillment of its outstanding obligations in the host State. However, such restriction is not included in the OIC Agreement. Further, in the UAA, the right to free transfer of capital is constrained by Article 7.3, which allows the host States to prevent national assets from exiting host State boundaries in accordance with any available procedure; "any recourse" is made available to the host State in these circumstances.[317] Article 11.4 of the OIC Agreement, contains a similar provision, but it does not extend the same discretion to host States as the UAA does. The OIC Agreement only allows the host State to follow currently existing exchange control measures for administrative purposes or to "prevent the illegal transfer abroad of the funds of its nationals."[318] In addition, the UAA (as adopted in 1981) and the OIC Agreement set out a time-limit before the expiry of which the investor is not entitled to retransfer the original capital of its investment. However, such time limit is not included in the amended UAA.

314 *Al-Warraq* (*supra* n 160) ¶¶ 554–555.
315 OIC Agreement (*supra* n 2) Art. 10.2(a).
316 Unified Arab Agreement (*supra* n 1) Art. 9.2.
317 Unified Arab Agreement (*supra* n 1) Art. 7.3.
318 OIC Agreement (*supra* n 2) Art. 11.4.

BLE 4 Comparing the protections of the OIC Agreement and the Unified Arab Agreement

	OIC Agreement	Unified Arab Agreement (1981)	Unified Arab Agreement (2013 Amendment)
otection Security	"The invested capital shall enjoy adequate protection and security and the host State shall give the necessary facilities and incentives to the investors engaged in activities therein." (Article 2)	"The States Parties … shall undertake to protect the investor, safeguard his investment and its related revenues and rights and, to the extent possible, to ensure the stability of the pertinent legal provisions." (Article 2)	"They [the States Parties] shall undertake to protect investors, investments and their revenues." (Article 2)
ee ansfer of pital	"The host State shall undertake to guarantee the free transfer to any contracting party of the capitals and its net proceeds in cash without the investor being subject to any discriminatory banking, administrative or legal restrictions and without any taxes or charges on the transfer." (Article 11.1)	"The Arab investor shall have the freedom to make periodic transfers … and of the revenues therefrom, and subsequently to make re-transfers to any State Party following settlement/fulfillment of his/her outstanding obligations without this being subject to any discriminatory banking, administrative or legal restrictions and without the transfer process incurring any taxes or duties." (Article 7.1)	"The Arab investor shall be free to transfer the invested capital and its revenues…, and subsequently re-transfer the same to any State Party without delay following settlement/fulfillment of his/her outstanding legal obligations arising from the investment project and owed to the host State; without this being subject to any discriminatory banking, administrative or legal restrictions and without the transfer process incurring any taxes or duties" (Article 6.1)

TABLE 4 Comparing the protections of the OIC Agreement and the Unified Arab Agreement (*cont.*)

	OIC Agreement	**Unified Arab Agreement (1981)**	**Unified Arab Agreement (2013 Amendment)**
National Treatment Clause	"The investor shall be accorded a treatment not less than that accorded by the host State to its national investors or others regarding the compensation of damage that may befall the physical assets of investment due to hostilities of international nature committed by any international body or due to civil disturbances or violent acts of general nature." (Article 14)	"[T]he capital of the Arab investor shall, without discrimination, be treated in the same manner as capital owned by the citizens of that State. It shall automatically acquire identical legal status in terms of rights, obligations, regulations and procedures, although this shall not apply to any additional concessions which the State Party may accord to an Arab investment." (Article 6.1)	"In the host State, invested Arab capital shall be treate in a manner not less favour able than the capital owne by the citizens of said State or a third State, whichever more favourable and witho discrimination." (Article 6.
Most-Favored-Nation Clause	"The investors of any contracting party shall enjoy, within the context of economic activity in which they have employed their investments in the territories of another contracting party, a treatment not less favourable than the treatment accorded to investors	No clear MFN clause. "The Arab investor shall, however, be entitled to opt for any other manner of treatment which is laid down in general provisions in force in the State where the investment is made under a law or an international agreement and which	"In the host State, invested Arab capital shall be treate in a manner not less favorable than the capital owne by the citizens of said State or a third State, whichever more favorable and withou discrimination." (Article 5.2 "The Arab investor shall be entitled to opt for any othe manner of treatment which is laid down in general

[TAB]LE 4 Comparing the protections of the OIC Agreement and the Unified Arab Agreement (*cont.*)

	OIC Agreement	**Unified Arab Agreement (1981)**	**Unified Arab Agreement (2013 Amendment)**
	belonging to another State not party to this Agreement, in the context of that activity and in respect of rights and privileges accorded to those investors." (Article 8.1) Exceptions: See Article 8.2 for narrow exceptions.	is applicable to a non-Arab investment in a similar field. This shall not include any privileged treatment accorded by the State in respect of specific projects which are of particular importance to that State." (Article 6.2) Exceptions: "privileged treatment accorded by the State in respect of specific projects which are of particular importance to that State." (Article 6.2)	provisions in force in the host State under any law, international agreement or other investment agreements." (Article 5.3) Exceptions: See Articles 5.3 and 5.4.
[Fa]ir and [Eq]uitable [Tr]eatment	-No FET provision -Importation of other FET provisions permitted through MFN provision in *Al-Warraq v. Indonesia*[319]	-No FET provision -No case law to date on possible importation of other FET provisions through MFN provision	"Arab capital in the State Party shall benefit from fair and equitable treatment at all times and shall not impose any Performance requirements or barriers to entry which could be harmful to investment or have a negative impact on it or its ownership." (Article 2)

[31]9 *Al-Warraq* (*supra* n 160) ¶ 555.

TABLE 4 Comparing the protections of the OIC Agreement and the Unified Arab Agreement (*cont.*)

	OIC Agreement	**Unified Arab Agreement (1981)**	**Unified Arab Agreement (2013 Amendment)**
Expropriation	"The host State shall undertake not to adopt or permit the adoption of any measure … if such a measure may directly or indirectly affect the ownership of the investor's capital or investment by depriving him totally or partially of his ownership, possession or utilization of his capital, or of his actual control…." (Article 10.1) Exception: Expropriations "in the public interest in accordance with the law, without discrimination and on prompt payment of adequate and effective compensation …" (Article 10.2)	"[T]he capital of the Arab investor shall not be subject to any specific or general measures … which wholly or partially affect any of the assets, reserves or revenues of the investor and which lead to confiscation, compulsory seizure, dispossession, nationalization, liquidation, dissolution, the extortion or elimination of secrets regarding technical ownership or other material rights, … or any other action which infringes the right of ownership itself…." (Article 9.1) Exception: Expropriations "for the public benefit in accordance with the authority vested in the State … provided that this is done on a non-discriminatory basis in return for fair compensation…." (Article 9.2(a))	"Invested Arab capital shal not be subject to any speci or general measures, …, which wholly or partially affect any of the assets, reserves or revenues of the invest or and which lead to…. or any other action which infringes the right o ownership itself or prejudices the intrinsic authorit of the owner in terms of hi her control and possession of the investment, his/her right to administer it, his/h acquisition of the revenue therefrom or the fulfilmen of his/her rights and the discharge of his/her obligations" (Article 8.1) Same exception but with further clarification on the damages: fair compensatio equal to the market value of the investment before making the expropriation decision to seize the property or it being made know to the public, whichever comes first. If it is not possible to verify the market value, compensation shall set in accordance with

LE 4 Comparing the protections of the OIC Agreement and the Unified Arab Agreement (*cont.*)

OIC Agreement	Unified Arab Agreement (1981)	Unified Arab Agreement (2013 Amendment)
		generally recognised principles for assessment and on the basis of equitable principles that take into consideration, inter alia, the investor's capital, depreciation, cost of replacement and other relevant factors..... If there is a delay in payment, interest shall be calculated on the compensation at the market rate, ..." (Article 8.2(a))

If the host State breached any of the above-mentioned standards/obligations, the Arab investor is entitled to claim a restoration of its investment to its state before the occurrence of the damage. If this is not possible, the investor is entitled to monetary compensation. This is regulated in detail under the provisions of the UAA and OIC which are straightforward and similar to their counterparts under traditional BITs.[320]

In addition to the above, it is worth mentioning that the UAA includes other distinct protections and privileges, such as the free movement of the Arab investor and his/her family members[321] and host State's obligation to assist in securing labour.[322]

320 Unified Arab Agreement (*supra* n 1) Art. 10 and 11; Unified Arab Agreement as Amended in 2013 (*supra* n 60) Art. 9 and 10; OIC Agreement (*supra* n 2) Art. 13.

321 Unified Arab Agreement (*supra* n 1) Art. 12; Unified Arab Agreement as Amended in 2013 (*supra* n 60) Art. 11.

322 Unified Arab Agreement (*supra* n 1) Art. 13; Unified Arab Agreement as Amended in 2013 (*supra* n 60) Art. 12.

6 Dispute Resolution

6.1 *The Unified Arab Agreement*

A key feature of the UAA is its dispute settlement mechanisms. For disputes arising under the Agreement, four principal methods of resolution are available: conciliation, arbitration, national courts of the host States and, importantly,

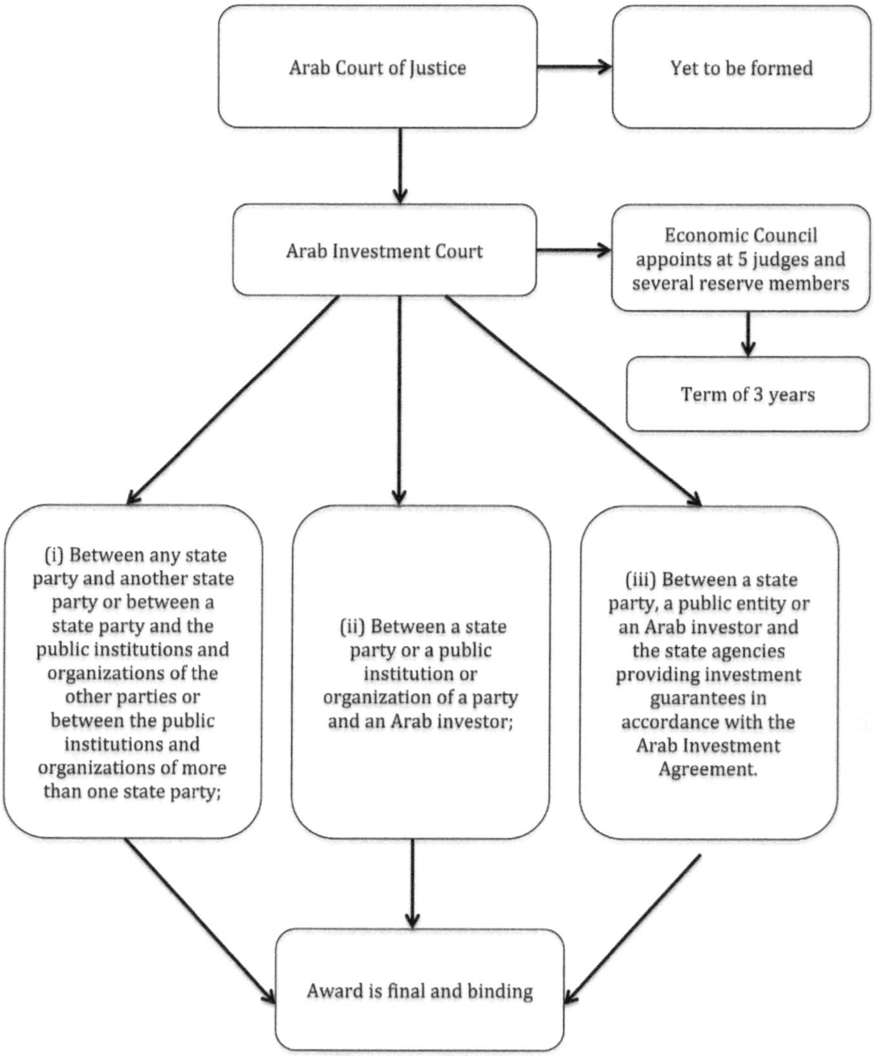

FIGURE 1A The dispute resolution mechanism under the Unified Arab Agreement *Arab Investment Court*

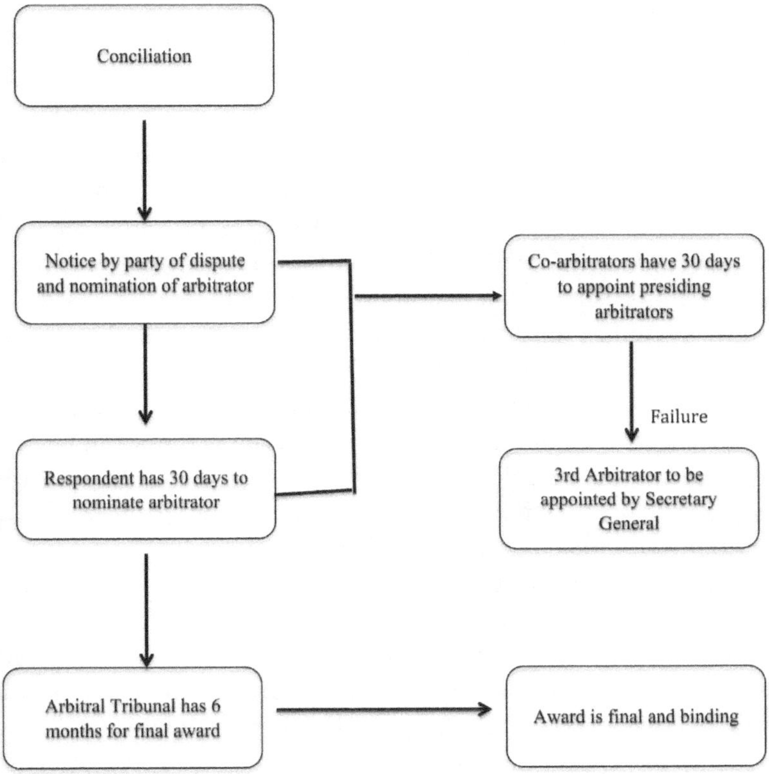

FIGURE 1B *Conciliation/Arbitration*

the Arab Investment Court (AIC), which began its operations in 2003.[323] In addition, the UAA amendments of 2013 further added mediation as a dispute settlement mechanism.

6.1.1 Conciliation and Mediation

The UAA (as adopted in 1981) includes conciliation as a dispute settlement mechanism, and, then came the UAA amendment of 2013 to further include the mediation. Remarkably, and unlike many BITs which only refer to mediation or conciliation, the UAA includes detailed regulation of mediation and conciliation procedures, which reflects an intent to support and encourage amicable settlement of disputes.

On a similar positive note, the UAA does not require parties to submit the dispute to mediation or conciliation for a certain period of time before

323 Mouawad & Khoury (*supra* n 36) 248; Unified Arab Agreement (supra n 1) Art. 25; Unified Arab Agreement as Amended in 2013 (*supra* n 60) Art. 23–24.

resorting to arbitration. This is also welcomed given the problems associated with imposing time-limits that may not work.

6.1.2 Arbitration

The UAA allows the parties to agree on arbitration. It states "the parties may agree to resort to arbitration", where they fail to agree to resort to conciliation, or where the conciliator proves unable to issue his/her report within the specified period, or where the parties did not agree on the conciliator's suggestions.[324]

The drafting of this provision may come across as unclear as to whether it constitutes a standing unequivocal consent of the contracting States to ad-hoc arbitration or whether the submission of the dispute to arbitration under the UAA requires a written consent from the States in a separate agreement.[325] On the reading of the text of the UAA, the latter position appears to be more favourable and this was indeed upheld, in *Al-Kharafi v. Libya* case, by the arbitral tribunal which based its jurisdiction to the dispute, arising under the UAA, on the arbitration clause in the agreement between the parties.[326]

From the publicly available documents, it appears that, at present, the arbitral award in *Al-Kharafi & Sons Co. v. Libya* is the only arbitral award ever issued pursuant to the UAA. In that case, Libya was ordered to pay US $935 million in damages to a Kuwaiti conglomerate for obstructing the investor's planned tourism development project in Libya.[327] The Libyan Ministry of Tourism approved Al-Kharafi & Sons Co.'s proposal for construction and operation of a tourism complex, which was slated to commence in 2007. After a delay in the project's start, the Ministry of Economy annulled the project's approval.

The claimant alleged that the Tourism Development Authority failed to hand over the property "free of occupancies and persons" as stipulated under the contract.[328] Local municipal guards allegedly assaulted the claimant when it attempted to build a fence and take over the land. According to the claimant, the Tourism Authority failed to evacuate the land and instead offered an

324 Annex "Conciliation and Arbitration" to the Unified Arab Agreement (*supra* n 1) Art. 2; Annex "Mediation, Conciliation and Arbitration" to the Unified Arab Agreement as Amended in 2013 (*supra* n 60) Art. 3.

325 Mouawad & Khoury (*supra* n 36) 250.

326 *Al-Kharafi & Sons Co. v. Libya*, Final Award, 22 March 2013, 391.

327 Vesel (*supra* n 73) 274.

328 *Al-Kharafi* (*supra* n 326) 22 ("The lessor undertook to hand over to the Plaintiff Company a plot of land free of occupancies and persons, or legal and physical impediments"); *see* Diana Rosert, "Libya ordered to pay US$935 million to Kuwaiti company for cancelled investment project; jurisdiction established under the Unified Agreement for the Investment of Arab Capital," (*Investment Treaty News*, 19 January 2014), https://www.iisd.org/itn/2014/01/19/awards-and-decisions-14/.

alternative plot of land. Libya subsequently annulled the project approval, which the claimant alleged was an "illegal act."[329] Libya challenged the jurisdiction of the tribunal on the ground that: (i) the project did not involve the transfer of Arab capital from Kuwait to Libya and the "substantial scope of the application of this Agreement is not fulfilled ipso facto," and (ii) the claim fell outside the limited scope of the arbitration clause in the contract.[330]

The tribunal, comprised of Dr. Abdel Hamid El-Ahdab as the presiding arbitrator, Dr. Ibrahim Fawzi, the claimant's nominated arbitrator, and Justice Mohamed El-Kamoudi El-Hafi, the Libyan nominated arbitrator, noted that the contract clause established consent to arbitration under the UAA and that the claimant's payment of 0.1% of the project value constituted a transfer of Arab Capital. The tribunal further found that it was competent to rule on the "scope of extension of the arbitration clause," which covered annulment of the contract and compensation for damages.[331] Libya argued that the claimant took the land free of any occupancy or impediments and was responsible for the delay in providing final project designs and a deposit of 10% of the project value in a Libyan bank account. These delays resulted in the lawful annulment of the approval.[332] Rejecting the allegation made by the Libyan authorities, the tribunal ruled that the Libyan authorities breached the contract by not providing the land "free of occupancies," which was evidenced, in part, by the fact that the authorities offered an alternative plot of land.[333] The tribunal further ruled that the annulment of the project approval was an "arbitrary decision" that led to confiscation, liquidation, and freezing of the project which was prohibited by Libyan Investment Law and Article 9(1) of the UAA.[334] The claimants were awarded US $935 million in damages which included lost profits and, moral damages, a rarity in international investment proceedings.[335]

In this regard, it is noteworthy that this award was subject to annulment/setting aside proceedings by Libya in Egypt, being the seat of arbitration. On

329 *Al-Kharafi* (*supra* n 326) 51.
330 *Al-Kharafi* (*supra* n 326) 66–67.
331 *Al-Kharafi* (*supra* n 326) 67.
332 *Al-Kharafi* (*supra* n 326) 71–77.
333 *See Al-Kharafi* (*supra* n 326) 286–288.
334 *Al-Kharafi* (*supra* n 326) 348 ("The Arbitral Tribunal considers that Decision No. 203/2010 issued by the Minister of Economy on 10/5/2010 and annulling the decision of the Minister of Tourism which approved the project, is an arbitrary decision and should be considered as a procedure similar to freezing and confiscation, both prohibited by virtue of Law No. 5 of 1997").
335 *Al-Kharafi* (*supra* n 326) 367–386 ("The Arbitral Tribunal has a discretionary power to determine the amount of compensation for direct moral and material damages and for lost profits").

11 June 2013, the Cairo Court of Appeal dismissed the annulment request on the basis of its lack of jurisdiction, in affirming that the UAA provides that the arbitral awards are unchallenged.[336] This is judgment was overturned by the Egyptian Court of Cassation on 4 November 2015.[337] However, for the second time, on 6 August 2018, the Cairo Court of Appeal held that it lacks jurisdiction over the dispute on the ground that the UAA provisions, being an international agreement, prevail over the Egyptian law and that the AIC would be the competent authority to rule on such request.[338] This judgment was also overturned by the Court of Cassation on 10 December 2019 on the ground that the Cairo Court of Appeal disregarded the Court of Cassation's res judicata ruling that the Cairo Court of Appeal has jurisdiction over the setting aside request of the awards issued under the UAA.[339] Accordingly, the Egyptian courts concluded that the UAA's provision that the arbitral awards rendered thereunder are final and binding does not preclude the proceedings of setting aside such awards before the Egyptian courts.

Subsequently, on 3 June 2020, the Cairo Court of Appeal annulled *Al-Kharafi* award on the basis that the proportionality principle and Egyptian public policy are violated by the arbitral tribunal which awarded exorbitant compensation that is grossly exaggerated beyond the loss sustained by Al-Kharafi.[340] This judgment was overturned by the Egyptian Court of Cassation, on 24 June 2021, which finally, after almost a decade, upheld the validity of *Al-Kharafi* award and put an end to *Al-Kharafi* saga.[341] In this judgment, "the Court of Cassation affirmed the longstanding principle that the role of the review courts is limited to examining the nullity of an arbitral award strictly based on the grounds set forth under Article (53) of the EAL [Egyptian Arbitration Law], and that these courts shall not conduct a de novo review of the merits, such that any error in the arbitral tribunal's assessment does not qualify as a ground for annulment given that a nullity action is not an appeal. Even if the arbitrators erred in the

336 Egyptian Cairo Court of Appeal, Challenge No. 39 of Judicial Year 130, Hearing Session dated 5 February 2014.

337 Egyptian Court of Cassation, Challenge No. 6065 of Judicial Year 84, Hearing Session dated 4 November 2015.

338 Cairo Court of Appeal, Challenge No. 39 of Judicial Year 130, Hearing Session dated 6 August 2018.

339 Egyptian Court of Cassation, Challenge No. 18615 of Judicial Year 88, Hearing Session dated 10 December 2019.

340 Cairo Court of Appeal, Challenge No. 39 of Judicial Year 130, Hearing Session dated 3 June 2020.

341 Egyptian Court of Cassation, Case No. 12262 of Judicial Year 90, Hearing Session dated 24 June 2021.

assessment of the amount for compensation or in the characterisation of the contract, this falls under the discretionary authority of the arbitral tribunal."[342]

With respect to the same issue of setting aside of *Al-Kharafi* award, Libya also filed this request before the AIC. In this respect, the AIC held, on 12 June 2014, that the requests for the setting aside of the arbitral awards do not fall within the jurisdiction of the AIC.[343] In addition to this reason, the AIC, in a further judgment rendered on 7 February 2017 regarding the same issue, confirmed its lack on jurisdiction over such request for setting aside of the award on the basis that the AIC is not an appeal court which may review the arbitral awards, and that it is not accorded the authority to set aside the awards in light of the express UAA provision that the arbitral awards are final and binding.[344] That said, unlike the Egyptian courts, the AIC concluded that the arbitral awards rendered under the UAA are final and shall not be subject to annulment proceedings.

In addition to the above well-known case, there are other few arbitration cases initiated under the UAA with no issued awards, which are *Ali Alyafei v. Hashemite Kingdom of Jordan*, Qatar Airways v. United Arab Emirates, Qatar Airways v. Saudi Arabia, Qatar Airways v. Egypt, Qatar Airways v. Bahrain.[345] In *Alyafei*, the claimant alleged that the Jordanian State violated the terms of a share purchase agreement with the claimant by not paying a contractually agreed "break-up fee" following his failure to acquire an interest in a Jordanian Bank.[346] The tribunal was comprised of Karl-Heinz Böckstiegel as the presiding

342 Mohamed S. Abdel Wahab & Noha Khaled Abdel Rahim, Mohamed Abdel Mohsen Al Kharafi & Sons Company for General Trade and Contracting v. (1) Libyan State, (2) Libyan Ministry of Economy, (3) the General Authority for Investment Promotion and Privatisation, (4) Libyan Ministry of Finance; and (5) Libyan Investment Authority, and (6) FINANCIERE CER Company, Court of Cassation of Egypt, Case No. 12262 of JY 90, 24 June 2021, A contribution by the ITA Board of Reporters, Kluwer Law International.

343 Arab Investment Court, Case No. 1 of Judicial Year 11, Hearing Session dated 12 June 2014.

344 Arab Investment Court, Case No. 3 Judicial Year 13, Hearing Session dated 7 February 2017.

345 Data gathered from UNCTAD Investment Dispute Settlement Navigator, https://investmentpolicy.unctad.org/investment-dispute-settlement.

346 *Ali Alyafei v. Hashemite Kingdom of Jordan*, ICSID Case No. ARB/15/24, Procedural Details, https://icsid.worldbank.org/en/Pages/cases/casedetail.aspx?CaseNo=ARB/15/24; Jarrod Hepburn & Luke Eric Peterson, *Investigation: As New Cases Emerge Under Islamic Investment Treaty, Initial Viability of Claims Seems to Hinge on Willingness of Respondents to Appoint Arbitrators*, IA REPORTER, Mar. 2, 2017, http://www.iareporter.com/articles/investigation-as-new-cases-emerge-under-islamic-investment-treaty-initial-viability-of-claims-seems-tohinge-on-willingness-of-respondents-to-appoint-arbitrators (subscription required) ("Qatari national Ali Alyafei alleges that the Jordanian State violated the terms of a share purchase agreement with the investor, by not paying a contractually-agreed 'break-up fee' following his failure to acquire an interest in a Jordanian bank").

arbitrator, Stephan Schill, nominated by the claimant, and Siegfried H. Elsing, nominated by Jordan. However, on July 11, 2016, on account of non-payment of the required advances, the tribunal dismissed the application on procedural grounds.[347] As noted below, the claimant thereafter initiated a new arbitration under the OIC Agreement.[348]

6.1.3 Arab Investment Court

The AIC is the default, but not exclusive, authority for the settlement of disputes under the UAA. The AIC has jurisdiction to hear investment disputes when the parties did not agree on another settlement mechanism or when the parties fail to accept decisions of the conciliator or fail to resort to agreed arbitration.[349] The AIC's constitution and jurisdiction as well as the procedures before it are regulated, in detail, under the UAA, the AIC's Statutes and the AIC's Bylaws.[350] It is seated at the permanent headquarters of the League of Arab States in Cairo.[351]

The AIC did not become operational until 2003 and did not issue its first decision until 2004, in *Tanmiah for Consultancy Management & Marketing v. Arab Republic of Tunisia*.[352] That case involved a dispute regarding the sponsorship of the Mediterranean Games held in Tunisia in September 2001. The claimant alleged that it entered into an agreement with the Tunisian Government for exclusive rights to the Games for television transmission and broadcasting, publicity operations, and ticket printing. The Tunisian Government violated the agreement, the claimant argued, by entering into a similar contract with a Tunisian company. The claimant further alleged that the Tunisian Government's sale of the space in the Olympic Village, refusal to deliver Olympic maps, failure to secure an insurance policy, and pursuit of a

---

347 *Ali Alyafei v. Hashemite Kingdom of Jordan*, ICSID Case No. ARB/15/24, Procedural Details, *supra* n 301) (" July 11, 2016 – The Tribunal issues an order taking note of the discontinuance of the proceeding for lack of payment of the required advances, pursuant to ICSID Administrative and Financial Regulation 14(3)(d).").

348 *See* Hepburn & Peterson (*supra* n 346) ("Mr. Alyafei initially turned to ICSID arbitration ... Mr. Alyafei then initiated a new arbitration, this time under the OIC Investment Treaty and ad-hoc auspices.").

349 Unified Arab Agreement (*supra* n 1) Art. 27; Unified Arab Agreement as Amended in 2013 (*supra* n 60) Art. 22.

350 The AIC's Statues and Bylaws are avaibale on the official website of the League of Arab States, http://www.leagueofarabstates.net/ar/legalnetwork/Pages/Investment_CourtSystems.aspx.

351 Unified Arab Agreement (*supra* n 1) Art. 28.

352 Mouawad & Khoury (*supra* n 36) 248.

negative campaign violated the agreement. The claimant sought US $68 million in monetary and moral damages. The Tunisian authorities alleged that the claimant did not spend or transfer money or make any regular payments stipulated under the agreement.[353] The AIC, comprised of Faiz Hassen El Mbiadh (President), Abdel Errahman Al Khalifa and Moubrak Nacer El Hajeri, held that the non-payment by the claimant to the Tunisian Government authorized the Tunisian authorities to "unilaterally repudiate the contract."[354] The AIC also rejected Tunisia's counterclaim.

Further, in the *Horizon Tourism vs. Egypt* case, the AIC dismissed Egypt's defense that claimant does not qualify as an investor due to the fact that the company in question is incorporated under the Egyptian law. The AIC considered that the claimant still qualifies as an investor on the basis that the shareholders are of the Saudi nationality and that the capital came from Saudi Arabia.[355]

In two other cases, the AIC held that it has no jurisdiction over the dispute filed by the investors against Egypt on the basis that their activities do not qualify as an investment contributing in Egypt's economic or social development neither under a specific agreement between Egypt and the investor nor under the Egyptian investment laws and regulations.[356]

In total, the AIC rendered to date 26 judgments, including 7 judgments in relation to requests for review of its judgments (requests for reconsideration) according to the public data available on the website of the League of Arab States.[357] It is noteworthy that none of these judgments granted the investor any of its claims.

Since the AIC's creation, other BITs have included adjudication by the Court as a dispute settlement option.[358] Similar to arbitration, AIC procedures are comparatively efficient, and disputes are resolved much faster than in national courts.[359] By the Agreement's terms, AIC judgments are binding and enforceable as if they were rendered in the country where enforcement is

353 Walid Ben Hamida, 'The First Arab Investment Court Decision' (2006) 7(5) J. WORLD INVESTMENT & TRADE 14–22.

354 Hamida (2006) (*supra* n 127) 719.

355 Arab Investment Court, Case No. 2 of Judicial Year 7, Hearing dated 27 April 2011.

356 Arab Investment Court, Case No. 1 of Judicial Year 17, Hearing dated 22 April 2014; Arab Investment Court, Case No. 4 of Judicial Year 17, Hearing dated 8 April 2021.

357 Arab Investment Court's Judgments are available on the official website of the League of Arab States, http://www.leagueofarabstates.net/ar/legalnetwork/Pages/Investment_CourtRulings.aspx.

358 Ziadé (*supra* n 41) 249, n. 59.

359 Kotb (*supra* n 56).

sought.[360] However, the AIC judgments may be subject to its review (a request for reconsideration) based on very restrictive grounds exhaustively listed under Article 35 of the UAA and Article 24 of the AIC's Bylaws.[361]

In addition to the foregoing, the AIC is granted the authority to issue an advisory opinion in relation to the issues falling within its jurisdiction upon request from the Secretary-General, a State Party or the Economic and Social Council of the League of Arab States.[362] In our opinion, this shall extend to include requests for advisory opinion from investors with a view of narrowing-down issues in dispute.[363]

6.1.4 National/Domestic Courts of the Host State

Besides the AIC's jurisdiction, the UAA grants the parties the option to submit their dispute to national courts of a host State.[364] Nonetheless, a party's choice between the AIC and national courts is final according to the "fork-in-the-road provision" enshrined in the UAA.[365] The scope of application of this "fork-in-the-road provision" is only relevant to the choice between the AIC and national courts. In other words, this provision is supposed not to apply to arbitration proceedings. Accordingly, the submission of an arbitration case does not preclude recourse to the AIC or national courts of the host State and vice-versa provided that the principle of res judicata is respected.[366] In case of a conflict of jurisdiction between the AIC and national courts of a host State, the AIC's decision on this matter shall be final pursuant to Article 32 of the UAA.[367]

360 The Amended Statutes of the Arab Investment Court, Art. 23.

361 Unified Arab Agreement (*supra* n 1) Art. 35; The Amended Bylaws of the Arab Investment Court, Art. 24.

362 Unified Arab Agreement (*supra* n 1) Art. 36; The Amended Bylaws of the Arab Investment Court, Art. 28.

363 Abdel Wahab (*supra* n 51) 67 ¶ 169.

364 Kotb (*supra* n 56) ("Both agreements [Unified Arab Agreement and the Amended Agreement] also provide a way to resolve disputes between the Arab investor and the host State, its public or local institutions or authorities, with respect to the application of the agreements. The Arab Investment Court (AIC) has jurisdiction, by default, over these disputes.") ("However, the parties are free to submit their investment dispute to the national courts of the host State"); Unified Arab Agreement (*supra* n 1) Art. 30; Unified Arab Agreement as Amended in 2013 (*supra* n 60) Art. 21.

365 Unified Arab Agreement (*supra* n 1) Art. 31; Unified Arab Agreement as Amended in 2013 (*supra* n 60) Art. 21.

366 Abdel Wahab (*supra* n 51) 50–51 ¶ 114.

367 Unified Arab Agreement (*supra* n 1) Art. 31.

6.2 *The OIC Agreement*

Article 17 of the OIC Agreement provides rules and procedures for settling disputes arising under the Agreement by either arbitration or conciliation. The Article specifies that arbitration and conciliation are available "[u]ntil an Organ for the settlement of disputes arising under the Agreement is established[.]"[368] However, the OIC has not yet developed an institution with the requisite jurisdiction and competence to displace arbitration under Article 17.[369] In 2009, the Islamic Centre for Development of Trade (ICDT), an OIC subsidiary group, confirmed the understanding that an organ within the meaning of Article 17 does not yet exist.[370] However, while there is general consensus that such organ does not yet exist, an older proposal to establish the International Islamic Court of Justice (IICJ) remains pending, and arbitration practitioners have disagreed sharply on the impact that its creation might have on current investments.[371]

At an October 2016 OIC meeting, the assembled foreign ministers issued a formal request for the Secretary General "to propose modalities for the creation of a permanent body for the settlement of disputes arising under" the OIC Agreement.[372] Since this request, a steering committee convened by the Secretary General has produced a nonpublic concept note setting out proposals for an Article 17 permanent body to displace arbitration. It is reported that such proposals would be set forth in a protocol subject to individual

368 OIC Agreement (*supra* n 2) Art. 17.1.

369 Hamida (2013) (*supra* n 78) 657–61 (the International Islamic Court of Justice does not qualify as the "organ" contemplated in the agreement).

370 Hamida (2013) (*supra* n 78) 661 ("In a note on the OIC Agreement presented by the ICDT ... it was recognized that 'the setting up of a dispute settlement organ will surely enhance the degree of confidence to guarantee the investment promotion and a better capital movement.'") (quoting Note on the Agreement on Investment Promotion, Protection and Guarantee concluded between the OIC Member States, presented by the Islamic Centre for Development of Trade to the 25th session of the Standing Committee for Economic and Commercial Cooperation of the OIC (COMCEC) in Istanbul, Republic of Turkey, 5–7 Nov. 2009).

371 Mouawad & Khoury (*supra* n 36) p. 258, n 75 (comparing Alison Ross & Kyriaki Karadelis, *An Arab Spring of Treaty Arbitration?*, GLOBAL ARB. REV., 24 February 2015, https://globalarbitrationreview.com/article/1034307/an-arab-spring-of-treaty-arbitration, with Hamida (2013) (*supra* n 78) 637, 638–39).

372 Joel Dahlquist & Luke Eric Peterson, *Governments Working to Rein in Use of OIC Investment Treaty's Investor-State Arbitration Offer*, IA REPORTER, 3 April 2019, https://www.iareporter.com/articles/governments-working-to-rein-in-use-of-oic-investment-treatys-investor-State-arbitration-offer/.

member-State adoption, rather than an amendment to the Agreement that would require consensus of four-fifths of the member States.[373]

Nevertheless, in the absence of such an organ, the principal three methods of dispute resolution under the OIC Agreement are national courts, conciliation and arbitration. In this respect, Article 16 of the OIC Agreement stipulates that "[t]he host state undertakes to allow the investor the right to resort to its national judicial system ...".[374] However, the same Article includes a "fork-in-the-road provision" which renders the party's choice between national courts of the host State and arbitration final.[375] Further, Article 17 of the OIC Agreement provides that "[u]ntil an Organ for the settlement of disputes arising under the Agreement is established, disputes that may arise shall be settled [sic] through conciliation or arbitration ..."[376]

More specifically, conciliation is available only if "the parties to the dispute agree on conciliation," whereas arbitration is made available by ensuring that "each party has the right to resort to the Arbitration Tribunal for a final decision on the dispute."[377] One party may initiate arbitration proceedings merely by providing the other with notice and naming its own arbitrator.[378] Upon receipt of the notice, the respondent party has sixty days to appoint its arbitrator and both the arbitrators have another sixty days to appoint an umpire. In the event the arbitrators fail to appoint an umpire, the OIC Secretary-General will be required to make the appointment.[379] Arbitral decisions are final and binding upon the parties.[380] Awards are enforceable, even against investors who are nationals or residents of non-member States.[381]

Given that the recourse to national courts of the host State and conciliation are clearly regulated under the OIC Agreement as mentioned above and given that there is no permanent organ for the settlement of the disputes arising from the OIC Agreement is established yet, the recourse to arbitration under the OIC Agreement remains a hot topic.

Unlike the UAA, the OIC Agreement includes the contracting States' consent to arbitration.[382] This is confirmed by the arbitral tribunal, in *Al-Warraq* case,

373 Dahlquist & Peterson (*supra* n 372).
374 OIC Agreement (*supra* n 2) Art. 16.
375 OIC Agreement (*supra* n 2) Art. 16.
376 OIC Agreement (*supra* n 2) Art. 17.
377 OIC Agreement (*supra* n 2) Art. 17.
378 OIC Agreement (*supra* n 2) Art. 17.2(b).
379 OIC Agreement (*supra* n 2) Art. 17.2(b).
380 OIC Agreement (*supra* n 2) Art. 17.2(d).
381 Hamida (2013) (*supra* n 78) 646.
382 OIC Agreement (*supra* n 2) Art. 17.2.

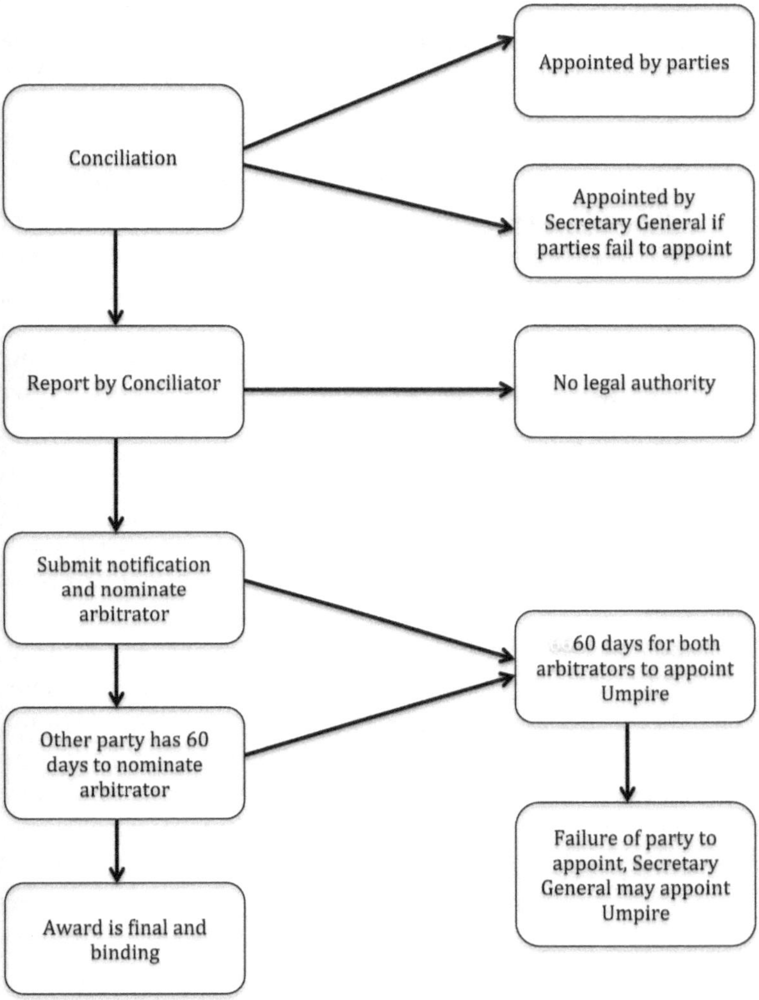

FIGURE 2 The dispute resolution mechanism under the OIC Agreement besides the national courts of the host State

which concluded that Article 17 of the OIC Agreement "established an effective investor-state dispute provision between the Contacting Parties and investors of other Contracting Parties" and that the Contracting Parties consented to arbitration under the OIC Agreement.[383]

383 Hesham T.M. Al Warraq v. Republic of Indonesia, UNCITRAL, Award on Respondent's Preliminary Objections to Jurisdiction and Admissibility of the Claims, 21 June 2012, ¶ 93.

Investors have faced some difficulties where countries have shirked responsibilities by avoiding their role in constituting an arbitral tribunal. Under the OIC Agreement, the OIC Secretary-General is the "default appointing authority," but according to some authors, the Secretary-General has often "failed to fulfil this role" by leaving the appointments to respondent States.[384] This allows respondent States to prevent the arbitral tribunal from even constituting.

In 2014, a Saudi businessman Hashem Al Mehdar and other members of his family initiated three arbitrations against Egypt in relation to their investments in Egypt's hotel and tourism sector. Egypt failed to appoint an arbitrator, and the OIC Secretary General did not make the default appointments when requested by the claimants to do so.[385] In 2017, the press reported that the claimant had abandoned his claims after he reached a settlement with Egypt.[386] As part of the settlement, it was reported that he was allowed to begin work on tourist projects that had previously been cancelled by Egypt.[387] However, more recent reports state that the claimant is currently pursuing a claim against Egypt under the OIC Agreement.[388] It is not clear whether the present claim pertains to assets separate from the ones covered under the purported settlement agreement.[389]

In *D.S. Construction FZCO v. Libya*, the Emirati claimant overcame the respondent State's failure to appoint an arbitrator.[390] In this case, the claimant was involved in construction projects in Libya, which were affected by the outbreak of the civil war in Libya in 2011.[391] The claimant argued that Libya's action or inaction after the outbreak of the civil war amounted to indirect expropriation, which resulted in losses amounting to US$525 million.[392] The claimant nominated Stanimir Alexandrov as arbitrator. After Libya refused

384 Vesel (*supra* n 73) p. 273.

385 Jarrod & Peterson (*supra* n 346).

386 Joel Dahlquist & Luke Eric Peterson, *Investigation: Four Previously-Confidential Claims under OIC Investment Agreement are Uncovered, as Controversy Continues over Treaty's Use in Arbitration*, IA REPORTER, 16 May 2019, https://www.iareporter.com/articles/investigation-4-previously-confidential-claims-under-oic-investment-agreement-are-uncovered-as-controversy-continues-over-treatys-use-in-arbitration/.

387 Dahlquist & Peterson (*supra* n 386).

388 Dahlquist & Peterson (*supra* n 386).

389 Dahlquist & Peterson (*supra* n 386).

390 Mouawad & Khoury (*supra* n 36) 263; Vesel (*supra* n 73) 273.

391 Alejandro A. Escobar & Dr. Ernesto Feliz De Jesus, *PCA Imports UNCITRAL Arbitral Rules Through MFN Clause to Designate an Appointing Authority in Arbitration Under Different Rules*, BAKER BOTTS, Oct. 25, 2017, http://www.bakerbotts.com/ideas/publications/2017/10/arbitration.

392 Escobar & De Jesus (*supra* n 391).

to appoint an arbitrator, the Emirati claimant, relying on the MFN clause to import Libya's consent to arbitrate under other agreements such as the Austria-Libya BIT (which provides for arbitration under the UNCITRAL Rules), petitioned the Permanent Court of Arbitration (PCA) Secretary-General to designate an appointing authority.[393] The claimant argued that the failure to appoint an arbitrator by the PCA Secretary-General would constitute a denial of justice, since it would effectively put an end to the arbitration proceedings.[394] Although Libya argued that the OIC Agreement did not permit the PCA to intervene, the PCA disagreed, holding itself competent under the 1976 UNCITRAL Rules to appoint an arbitrator.[395] The PCA nominated a former ICSID Deputy Secretary-General Nassib Ziadé as arbitrator, and both arbitrators then appointed a former judge of the International Court of Justice, Bruno Simma, as tribunal chairman.[396] This decision by the PCA appeared to potentially have opened the door to wider use of the OIC Agreement's dispute settlement provisions; however, in March 2021, the Paris Court of Appeal concluded that the tribunal was improperly constituted, annulling a preliminary award rendered by the tribunal finding that it was validly constituted.[397] Though the decision by the Court of Appeal may still be appealed to the French *Cour de Cassation*, the decision casts doubt on the viability of other proceedings against Libya as well as of arbitration under the OIC Agreement more generally.[398]

That being said, the host State and the Secretary-General's abstention from appointing an arbitrator remains a serious unresolved issue threatening the investors' right to pursue their claims in arbitration under the OIC Agreement.

Notwithstanding the above issue, there are 16 known arbitration cases filed under the OIC Agreement.[399] The OIC Agreement had not been invoked in arbitration cases for decades, but recently, has been the basis of several ad-hoc arbitration cases.[400]

---

393 Mouawad & Khoury (*supra* n 36) 263; Vesel (*supra* n 73) 273.

394 Mouawad & Khoury (*supra* n 36) 26.

395 Mouawad & Khoury (*supra* n 36).

396 Escobar & Feliz De Jesus (*supra* n 391).

397 *See* Damien Charlotin, *Breaking: Paris Court Finds That PCA Secretary General Lacked Power to Step into Libya Arbitration When OIC Secretary General Failed to Appoint Arbitrator*, IA REPORTER, 26 March 2021, https://www.iareporter.com/articles/breaking-paris-court-finds-that-pca-secretary-general-lacked-power-to-step-into-libya-arbitration-when-oic-secretary-general-failed-to-appoint-arbitrator/.

398 *See id.*

399 Data gathered from UNCTAD Investment Dispute Settlement Navigator, https://investmentpolicy.unctad.org/investment-dispute-settlement.

400 Ziadé (2017) (*supra* n 266) 50.

The first case in which the arbitration provision under the OIC Agreement was invoked, for the first time, is *Al-Warraq* case in 2011.[401] The claimant in *Al-Warraq*, a shareholder of Indonesia's third largest bank, brought claims for expropriation and breach of fair and equitable treatment, alleging that Indonesia had used designated bail-out funds to finance the presidential election campaign.[402] The claimant argued that the treatment of his investment breached the OIC Agreement's provisions on expropriation and adequate protection and security, and that the manner in which the criminal investigation and prosecution were conducted breached the claimant's right to fair and equitable treatment.[403] Indonesia, on the other hand, argued that the claimant's acts were prejudicial to the public interest and that this breached the OIC Agreement. Indonesia also filed a counterclaim for US$360 million.[404] The tribunal – comprised of Michael Hwang SC as the claimant's nominee, Fali Nariman as Indonesia's nominee, and chaired by Bernardo Cremades – agreed with the claimant that Indonesia violated due process in the criminal proceedings against the claimant and breached the fair and equitable treatment standard as well as Indonesia's obligations under the International Covenant on Civil and Political Rights of 1966.[405] However, the tribunal dismissed the claim on account of its finding of various fraudulent acts taken by the claimant in the course of the investment.[406] The tribunal concluded that the claimant's actions were "prejudicial to the public interest" and the claims therefore could not proceed due to the claimant's "unclean hands."[407]

In *Kontinental Conseil Ingénierie v. Gabonese Republic*, a Tunisian investor initiated, in 2015, an arbitration against Gabon over the alleged destruction of a social housing construction investment.[408] There is little information available about this case due to confidentiality arrangements but, from what is known, the claimant asserted that it had been awarded a contract in 2011 to build 5000 houses at a site near Libreville. The contract formed part of an extensive program of social housing construction launched by the Gabonese President in July 2009, aimed at improving the country's development status.[409] The claimant alleged that after the construction work commenced in 2011, a

401 Mouawad & Khoury (*supra* n 36) 254.
402 *Al-Warraq* (*supra* n 160) ¶¶ 99–112.
403 *Al-Warraq* (*supra* n 160) ¶¶ 122–127.
404 *Al-Warraq* (*supra* n 160) ¶¶ 137–146.
405 *Al-Warraq* (*supra* n 160) ¶ 195.
406 *Al-Warraq* (*supra* n 160) ¶¶ 634–648.
407 Mouawad & Khoury (*supra* n 36) 251.
408 Mouawad & Khoury (*supra* n 36).
409 Jarrod & Peterson (*supra* n 346).

change in the Minister of Housing after elections in 2012 led to difficulties. Gabon not only failed to make an advance payment for the construction work as required under the contract, but also issued an arbitrary order to cease work on the construction site. This suspension was never lifted and, despite negotiations with the new Minister of Housing, the issue was not resolved. Ultimately, the claimant initiated arbitration and a tribunal was constituted nominated Nassib Ziadé. Gabon nominated French professor Mathias Audit, and both the arbitrators nominated Pierre Mayer to chair the proceedings. Reports indicate that the tribunal found Gabon liable for unfair treatment, but did not award the compensation sought.[410] Reportedly, only 4.3 million EUR was awarded against a demand of more than 240 million EUR.[411] In June 2019, the Paris Court of Appeal upheld the award, after the claimant sought to have parts of it annulled.[412] It is noteworthy that, according to the available data, this is the only award issued in favor of the investor under the OIC Agreement.[413]

Further, in 2015, a Qatari investor filed an arbitration case against Jordan under the OIC Agreement, which is *Ali Alyafei v. Hashemite Kingdom of Jordan* case. This case – as noted above – was first initiated by the claimant under the Unified Arab Agreement but was discontinued. The claimant thereafter initiated a new arbitration under the OIC Agreement. The tribunal was constituted with the French arbitrator Pierre Mayer as the presiding arbitrator, Laurence Boisson de Chazournes as the claimant's nominee, and Paolo Michele Patocchi as the nominee of Jordan. The arbitration was subsequently discontinued.[414]

In 2017, a case was filed against Iraq, by Dubai-based VTEL Holdings and Itisaluna Iraq, along with other affiliates, which is discussed *supra* Part 4.3.[415] The claimants invoked the Japan-Iraq BIT to import certain provisions under the Japan-Iraq treaty (including the State's consent to ICSID jurisdiction) through the OIC Agreement's MFN provision, much like in *Al-Warraq*. However, the ICSID tribunal concluded that it has no jurisdiction over the dispute on the basis that the MFN clause may not be relied upon to establish the host State's consent to ICSID arbitration included in another BIT.

410 Jarrod & Peterson (*supra* n 346).

411 Dahlquist & Peterson (*supra* n 386).

412 *See* Damien Charlotin, *Foreign Investor Fails in Bid to Annul OIC Investment Treaty Award's Damages Holdings*, IA REPORTER, 26 June 2019, https://www.iareporter.com/articles/foreign-investor-fails-in-bid-to-annul-oic-investment-treaty-award/.

413 Data gathered from UNCTAD Investment Dispute Settlement Navigator, https://investmentpolicy.unctad.org/investment-dispute-settlement.

414 *See* Hepburn & Peterson (*supra* n 346).

415 *Itisaluna Iraq LLC, Munir Sukhtian International Investment LLC, VTEL Holdings Ltd., VTEL Middle East and Africa Limited v. Republic of Iraq*, ICSID Case No. ARB/17/10, Final Award, 3 April 2020.

Another case involving an award issued in favor of the host State is *Navodaya Trading DMCC v. Gabonese Republic* and was decided in December 2020. Navodaya instituted its claims against Gabon for not renewing the permit previously granted to Navodaya for manganese exploration in East Gabon.[416] Gabon alleged that Navodaya failed to comply with its obligations.[417] Navodaya asserted that it was in compliance, and seeks the value of its lost investment.[418] Gabon appointed Laurent Aynes to the arbitration panel, whereas Navodaya appointed Stanimir Alexandrov, with Gabrielle Kaufman-Kohler chairing the case.[419] It is reported that the tribunal has already rendered (unpublished) decisions on provisional measures and jurisdiction.[420]

In addition to the above cases, there are other pending and discontinued arbitration cases filed under the OIC Agreement. Two cases have been brought by Qatari firms against Saudi Arabia. In October 2018, Qatari media firm beIN Corporation filed a request for arbitration alleging breaches of the OIC Agreement's adequate protection and security, expropriation, free transfer of capital, and nondiscrimination clauses; the firm relies on the Agreement's MFN clause to import standards of fair and equitable treatment and full protection and security from the Saudi Arabia-Austria BIT.[421] The claimant also relies on this BIT to seek the procedural protections of the UNCITRAL rules – including having the Secretary-General of the PCA act as appointing authority – rather than the OIC Agreement's own provisions.[422] In March 2019, meanwhile, another Qatari firm, Qatar Pharma, filed a request for arbitration against Saudi Arabia, alleging that Saudi measures have led to a loss of access to the firm's Saudi facilities.[423]

---

416 Dahlquist & Peterson (*supra* n 386).

417 Dahlquist & Peterson (*supra* n 386).

418 Dahlquist & Peterson (*supra* n 386).

419 Dahlquist & Peterson (*supra* n 386).

420 Dahlquist & Peterson (*supra* n 386).

421 Jarrod Hepburn, *Saudi Arabia Faces $1 Billion Claim by Qatari Media Firm Under OIC Investment Agreement, Amidst Gulf Diplomatic Crisis*, IA REPORTER, 1 October 2018, https://www.iareporter.com/articles/saudi-arabia-faces-1-billion-claim-by-qatari-media-firm-under-oic-investmentagreement-amidst-gulf-diplomatic-crisis/; *see also beIN Corporation v. Kingdom of Saudi Arabia*, UNCITRAL ad hoc, Notice of Arbitration, 1 Oct. 2018.

422 *See beIN Corporation*, Notice of Arbitration (*supra* n 352); *see also* Luke Eric Peterson, *OIC Round Up: An Update on Pending Arbitration Cases Lodged Under the OIC Investment Agreement*, IA REPORTER, 11 Aug. 2020, https://www.iareporter.com/articles/oic-round-up-an-update-on-pending-arbitration-cases-lodged-under-the-oic-investment-agreement/.

423 Luke Eric Peterson, *Saudi Arabia Faces Another Investor Arbitration Claim Under Organisation for Islamic Cooperation Investment Treaty – Brought by Qatari Pharma Firm*

There are two ongoing OIC Agreement arbitration cases filed against Libya. In the first, an Emirati firm, Trasta Energy, filed a claim against Libya under the OIC Agreement in January 2019. The claim is the latest in a long-running dispute between Trasta and Libya's National Oil Corporation in the aftermath of a joint venture to operate a refinery.[424] The dispute has been subject to ongoing proceedings at the International Chamber of Commerce (ICC), as well.[425] The second case is *D.S. Construction FZCO v. Libya* with the issue of lack of appointment of an arbitrator by the host State, which is further discussed above in this section.

In a further case, a Saudi investor, Dr. Hilal Hussain Al-Tuwairqi, and an entity he controls, brought claims under the OIC Agreement against Pakistan arising out of investment in a Pakistani steel plant.[426] The dispute related to the price of gas offered and the flow of electricity to the facility.[427] The case was reportedly instituted in 2018 in London, with initial briefs on the question of jurisdiction already filed.[428] The claimant appointed John Beechey, the State appointed H.N Judge Awn Al-Khasawneh, with Salim Moollan QC as the chair.[429]

In addition to the above, there are other pending arbitration cases filed under the OIC Agreement, namely *Bin Sulaiman v. Oman, Al Mehdar v. Egypt* (discussed above), *Qatar Airways v. United Arab Emirates, Qatar Airways v. Saudi Arabia, Qatar Airways v. Egypt, Qatar Airways v. Bahrain*.[430]

The early record of dispute resolution through arbitration under the OIC Agreement is mixed. On the one hand, investors have been stymied by the lack of established procedures for appointment of a tribunal in several cases. On the other hand, a growing number of cases are resolving initial jurisdictional

---

Affected by Blockade, IA REPORTER, 29 March 2019, https://www.iareporter.com/articles/saudi-arabia-faces-another-investor-arbitration-claim-under-organisation-for-islamic-cooperation-investment-treaty/.

424 Jarrod Hepburn & Luke Eric Peterson, *As Another Claim Is Filed Against Libya Under OIC Investment Agreement, Government Goes to Court to Try to Block PCA-Enabled Arbitrations Under Treaty*, IA REPORTER, 13 Jan. 2019, https://www.iareporter.com/articles/as-another-claim-is-filed-against-libya-under-oic-investment-agreement-government-goes-to-court-to-try-to-block-pca-enabled-arbitrations-under-treaty/.

425 Aidan Lewis, *Differences Between Operator, NOC Cloud Hopes for Restart at Libya Refinery*, REUTERS, 15 January 2018, https://af.reuters.com/article/libyaNews/idAFL8N1PA34G.

426 Dahlquist & Peterson (*supra* n 386).

427 Dahlquist & Peterson (*supra* n 386).

428 Dahlquist & Peterson (*supra* n 386).

429 Dahlquist & Peterson (*supra* n 386).

430 Data gathered from UNCTAD Investment Dispute Settlement Navigator, https://investmentpolicy.unctad.org/investment-dispute-settlement.

and procedural challenges and adjudicating cases on the merits. As more cases establish precedent for overcoming these early hurdles, the OIC Agreement may become an increasingly important vehicle for encouraging and protecting investment in the Muslim world.

It is also worth mentioning that, as noted above, the newly proposed procedures to be adopted under the OIC Agreement, as presented by Dr. Kane, appointed by the OIC as a "Project Manager", include several steps which an aggrieved investor should follow before commencing investment arbitration proceedings.[431] Briefly, an investor must first exhaust local remedies, and, then, it should request its home State to amicably settle the issue with the host State.[432] If State-to-State talks fail, the investor may file a claim before a First Instance Panel, and the Panel's decision may be appealed before an Appellate Committee.[433]

6.3 *Comparison of the Agreements' Approaches to Dispute Resolution*

There are a few key differences between the OIC Agreement and the Unified Arab Agreement regarding dispute resolution.

First, unlike the UAA, the OIC Agreement contains an advance consent by its contracting States to ad-hoc arbitration. Although there was some initial debate over whether Article 17 of the OIC Agreement provided State consent to arbitration (a "slightly confusing" English version of the Agreement may be responsible for causing that confusion, the French and Arabic versions demonstrate manifest State consent).[434] The majority in *Itisaluna v. Iraq* interpreted Articles 16 and 17 of the OIC Agreement as providing for investor-State arbitration, but noted that attempted conciliation between the parties is a condition precedent.

The UAA, on the other hand, does not contain such advance consent by its contracting States to arbitration, which requires the Arab investors to obtain the host State's consent to arbitration from a separate investment agreement/contract. This is confirmed by the arbitral tribunal's approach in *Al-Kharafi & Sons Co. v. Libya* case in which the tribunal relied on an arbitration clause in the contract between the host State and the investor to declare its jurisdiction over the dispute.

Second, the UAA established and led to the creation of the AIC, whereas the institutional organ envisioned by the OIC Agreement has not yet been formed. Currently, there is a clear preference for arbitration under the OIC Agreement,

431 Kumtepe (2019) (*supra* n 74), Slide 9.
432 Kumtepe (2019) (*supra* n 74), Slide 9.
433 Kumtepe (2019) (*supra* n 74), Slide 9.
434 Mouawad & Khoury (*supra* n 36) 258.

given the UAA's limitations described above. But unless the OIC Agreement is amended explicitly to guarantee the continued availability of conciliation and arbitration, Article 17 suggests that the creation of an inter-Islamic court would swallow all disputes under the OIC Agreement.

7 Conclusion

The Unified Arab Agreement and the OIC Agreement each serve to foster economic cooperation and development in the Arab and Muslim-majority worlds, respectively. They provide investment guarantees within a diverse and expansive territory that is of primordial importance to international politics and the global economy. The two treaties overlap in significant ways, both in the territory they cover and the guarantees they provide to foreign investors. However, the agreements do present meaningful differences. While these differences may seem minor at first blush, they could potentially produce disparate levels of protection that should be considered closely.

In some ways the UAA, in particular the version amended in 2013, provides more protection to investors than the OIC Agreement, including through seemingly broader provisions on full protection and security, national treatment and fair and equitable treatment. This relative strength will be reinforced if the proposed OIC Agreement amendments are adopted, since the proposal significantly weakens investors' ability to successfully bring suit against member States. The OIC Agreement, however, is perhaps stronger with regard to the standard of compensation due in the event of expropriation and with respect to the re-transfer of capital and revenues.

Meanwhile, both agreements' dispute resolution procedures remain in a developmental stage. The UAA does not include an express consent to arbitration by its contracting States, but instead, it only allows the parties to agree on arbitration in a separate agreement/contract, which reduces the chances of resorting to arbitration under the UAA. Equally, the eventual creation of an inter-Islamic court would cause similar uncertainty over the durability of the OIC Agreement's guarantees and the recourse to arbitration under the said Agreement. Moreover, the host States and the OIC Secretary-General's abstention from appointing an arbitrator in the arbitration cases filed by the investors under the OIC Agreement constitutes a serious issue which may jeopardise the OIC system. Accordingly, this issue merits careful consideration by OIC member States which should urge the OIC Secretary-General to carry out his/her duty of appointing the arbitrator on behalf of the host State abstaining from doing so.

Furthermore, the establishment of a permanent organ for the dispute settlement under the OIC Agreement – which has been awaited for decades – has not been implemented to date. The equivalent organ under the UAA, i.e. AIC, is established and in operation, but the AIC has not yet established itself as an organ with coherent and clear case law attractive to investors. To date, the investors seem to prefer the recourse to arbitration over the AIC. Such preference may be due to the fact that, out of the 26 judgments rendered by the AIC, none of them was in favor of the investor. Most importantly, the selection of AIC judges merits due consideration to ensure that appointees to the AIC are fully independent, well-versed in international law issues and well-experienced in deciding investment disputes.

In addition to the foregoing, it is worth mentioning that the lack of ratification of the amended UAA by many Arab States gives rise to a complex and undesirable situation where the old and new versions of the same treaty coexist. The UAA (as amended in 2013) would apply only to disputes where both parties to the dispute are nationals of States which have ratified the amendment, while, till date, the original UAA (as adopted in 1981) remains in effect to govern disputes where one of the parties is national of a State which had not ratified the said amendment.

In light of the above, it is more important than ever that stakeholders gain a mastery of the provisions of the two agreements. Arab and Muslim investors will need to advocate for themselves in the amendment processes, and to do so effectively will require a clear understanding of two investment regimes. The same principle holds true for UAA and OIC member States, whose traditional roles as global capital-importing and capital-exporting States may shift in the context of treaties confined to the Arab and Muslim worlds. These States may decide to recalibrate their preferred balance between the competing goals of sovereignty and investor protection.

Bibliography

Laws/Draft Rules

Draft Arbitration Rules on Business and Human Rights, The Hague Rules on Business and Human Rights Arbitration.

Elements for Consideration in Draft Arbitral Rules, Model Clauses, and Other Aspects of the Arbitral Process, The Hague Rules on Business and Human Rights Arbitration.

Books

Filip Balcerzak, Investor–State Arbitration and Human Rights (2017).

Pierre-Marie Dupuy, Ernst-Ulrich Petersmann, & Francesco Francioni, Human Rights in International Investment Law and Arbitration (2009).

Yannick Radi, Research Handbook on Human Rights and Investment (2018).

Journal/Book Articles

Adam H. Bradlow, Human Rights Impact Litigation in ISDS: A Proposal for Enabling Private Parties to Bring Human Rights Claims Through Investor-State Dispute Settlement Mechanisms, Yale Journal of International Law 43 (2) 355–390 (2018).

Angelo Golia, Enforcing Human Rights Through Constitutional Law in Investor-State Arbitration: An Alternative Approach to Pacific Rim v. El Salvador, Human Rights & International Legal Discourse 11 (2) 182–221 (2017).

Bruno Simma, Foreign Investment Arbitration: A Place For Human Rights?, The International and Comparative Law Quarterly 60 (3) 573–596 (2011).

Chang-fa Lo, Normative and Operational Linkages Between Human Rights Law and BITs – Building a Firmer Status of Human Rights in Investor-State Arbitration, Contemporary Asia Arbitration Journal 8 (1) 1–28 (May 2015).

Cynthia M. Ho, Reexamining Eli Lilly v. Canada: A Human Rights Approach to Investor-State Disputes?, Vanderbilt Journal of Entertainment and Technology Law 21 (2) 437–482 (2018).

Daniel Gervais, Investor-State Dispute Settlement: Human Rights and Regulatory Lessons from Lilly v. Canada, UC Irvine Law Review 8 459–511 (2018).

Enrique Boone Barrera, Property Rights as Human Rights in International Investment Arbitration: A Critical Approach, Boston College Law Review 59 (8) 2635–2662 (Nov 2018).

Eric De Brabandere, Human Rights Considerations in International Investment Arbitration, in The Interpretation and Application of the European Convention of Human Rights: Legal and Practical Implications (ed. Malgosia Fitzmaurice and Panos Merkouris) 1–27 (2013).

Ernst-Ulrich Petersmann, Human Rights, Constitutionalism, And 'Public Reason' In Investor-State Arbitration in International Investment Law for the 21st Century: Essays in Honour of Christoph Schreuer (ed. Christina Binder, Ursula Kriebaum, August Reinisch, and Stephan Wittich) (2009).

Filip Balcerzak, Determination of Compensation in Investor-State Arbitrations: Is There a Place for Human Rights Considerations?, Frontiers of International Economic Law: Legal Tools to Confront Interdisciplinary Challenges (2016).

Fola Adeleke, Human Rights And International Investment Arbitration, South African Journal on Human Rights 32 (1) 48–70 (2016).

Henok Gabisa, The Fate of International Human Rights Norms in the Realm of Bilateral Investment Treaties (BITs): Has Humanity Become a Collateral Damage?, The International Lawyer 48(2) 153–167 (2014).

James D. Fry, International Human Rights Law In Investment Arbitration: Evidence Of International Law's Unity, Duke Journal of Comparative and International Law 18 77–149 (2007).

Jasper Krommendijk & John Morijn, 'Proportional' by What Measure(s)? Balancing Investor Interests and Human Rights by Way of Applying the Proportionality Principle in Investor-State Arbitration, in Human Rights in International Investment Law and Arbitration (ed. Pierre-Marie Dupuy, Ernst-Ulrich Petersmann, and Francesco Francioni), 421–455 (OUP:2009).

Jose E. Alvarez, The Use (and Misuse) of European Human Rights Law by Investor-State Arbitrators in The Boundaries of Investment Arbitration (ed. Jose E. Alvarez) (Sept 2018).

Lorenzo Cotula, Human Rights And Investor Obligations In Investor-State Arbitration, Journal of World Investment and Trade 17 (1) 148–157 (2016).

Luke Eric Peterson & Kevin R. Gray, International Human Rights in Bilateral Investment Treaties and in Investment Treaty Arbitration, International Institute For Sustainable Development (2003).

Maggie Ng, Can Human Rights Counterclaims Succeed in Investment Treaty Arbitration?, Transnational Dispute Management (5) (2018), available at www.transnational-dispute-management.com/article.asp?key=2600.

Markus Krajewski, Human Rights in International Investment Law: Recent Trends in Arbitration and Treaty-Making Practice (2018).

Mohamed S. Abdel Wahab, *A Study on the Unified Agreement for the Investment of Arab Capital*, World Journal of Arbitration, 17 (2013).

Mohamed S. Abdel Wahab, *Itisaluna and Others v Iraq: The OIC Agreement Conundrum: Consent to ICSID Arbitration and the MFN Clauses Saga*, ICSID Review, 1–13 (2020).

Mohamed S. Abdel Wahab & Noha Khaled Abdel Rahim, Mohamed Abdel Mohsen Al Kharafi & Sons Company for General Trade and Contracting v. (1) Libyan State, (2) Libyan Ministry of Economy, (3) the General Authority for Investment Promotion and Privatisation, (4) Libyan Ministry of Finance; and (5) Libyan Investment Authority, and (6) FINANCIERE CER Company, Court of Cassation of Egypt, Case No. 12262 of JY 90, 24 June 2021, A contribution by the ITA Board of Reporters, Kluwer Law International.

Monica Feria-Tinta, Like Oil and Water? Human Rights in Investment Arbitration in the Wake of *Philip Morris v. Uruguay*, Journal of International Arbitration 601–630 (2017).

Nicolette Butler & Shavana Musa, Systemizing Human Rights Within Investment Arbitration, American Review of International Arbitration 28 (4) (2017).

Patrick Dumberry & Gabrielle Dumas-Aubin, How to Impose Human Rights Obligations on Corporations Under Investment Treaties?, Yearbook on International Investment Law and Policy, 2011–2012 4 569–600 (2014).

Patrick Dumberry & Gabrielle Dumas-Aubin, The Doctrine of 'Clean Hands' and the Inadmissibility of Claims by Investors Breaching International Human Rights Law, Transnational Dispute Management Special Issue: Aligning Human Rights and Investment Protection 10 (1) 1–10 (2013).

Patrick Dumberry, When and How Allegations of Human Rights Violations Can Be Raised in Investor-State Arbitration, Journal of World Investment & Trade 13(3) 349–372 (2012).

Petra Butler, Red Riding Hood – Is Investor-State Arbitration the Big Bad Wolf?, 5 Penn State Journal of Law & International Affairs 328 (2017).

Rodrigo Polanco Lazo & Rodrigo Mella, Investment Arbitration And Human Rights Cases In Latin America, Research Handbook on Human Rights and Investment 41–92 (2018).

Sarah Schadendorf, Human Rights Arguments in Amicus Curiae Submissions: Analysis of ICSID and NAFTA Investor-State Arbitrations, Transnational Dispute Management Special Issue: Aligning Human Rights and Investment Protection 10 (1) 1–23 (2013).

Siddharth S. Aatreya, Human Rights and the ISDS Regime – Rethinking the Bipartisan Structure of International Investment Arbitrations, Gonzaga Journal of International Law 22 (1) 28–49 (2018).

Silvia Steininger, What's Human Rights Got To Do With It? An Empirical Analysis of Human Rights References in Investment Arbitration, Leiden Journal of International Law 31 (1) 33–58 (2018).

Susan Karamanian, The Role of International Human Rights Law in Re-Shaping Investor-State Arbitration. International Journal of Legal Information 45(1), 34–41 (2017).

Susan L. Karamanian, The Place of Human Rights in Investor-State Arbitration, Lewis and Clark Law Review 17 (2) 423–447 (2013).

Tamar Meshel, Human Rights in Investor-State Arbitration: The Human Right to Water and Beyond, Journal of International Dispute Settlement (2015).

Ursula Kriebaum, Is ISDS Beneficial or Dangerous for the Rule of Law Both in the International and the National Spheres?, Proceedings of the Annual Meeting (American Society of International Law) 109 203–207 (2015).

Vivian Kube & Ernst-Ulrich Petersmann, Human Rights Law in International Investment Arbitration, Asian Journal of WTO & International Health Law and Policy 11 (1) 66–113 (2016).

W. Ben Hamida, Investment Arbitration and Human Rights, TRANSNATIONAL DISPUTE MANAGEMENT (5) (2018), available at www.transnational-dispute-management.com/article.asp?key=1142.

Reports

Committee on Legal Affairs and Human Rights, Human Rights Compatibility Of Investor-State Arbitration In International Investment Protection Agreements, PARLIAMENTARY ASSEMBLY FOR THE COUNCIL OF EUROPE AS/Jur (2016) 32.

Impacts of the International Investment Regime on Access to Justice, UN WORKING GROUP ON BUSINESS AND HUMAN RIGHTS (2018).

International Arbitration Of Business and Human Rights Disputes, THE WORKING GROUP ON INTERNATIONAL ARBITRATION OF BUSINESS AND HUMAN RIGHTS (2017).

UNCTAD, Reforming Investment Dispute Settlement: A Stocktaking (March 2019).

UNCTAD, Selected Recent Developments in IIA Arbitration and Human Rights, IIA MONITOR 2 (2009).

Press Articles/Web Articles

Akshay Sewlikar, Introduction of Labour Standards in Investment Arbitration, KLUWER ARBITRATION BLOG, available at http://arbitrationblog.kluwerarbitration.com/2014/03/18/introduction-of-labour-standards-in-investment-arbitration/ (Mar. 18, 2014).

Amanda Neil, Ella Davies & Will Thomas (Freshfields Bruckhaus Deringer LLP), Human rights and investment arbitration: What we can expect in 2019, LEXOLOGY, available at https://www.lexology.com/library/detail.aspx?g=6bc68074-ca1c-41c9-9ce4-a251acbd8fe2 (Mar. 8, 2019).

An Open Letter To The Chair Of UNCITRAL Working Group III And To All Participating States Concerning The Reform Of The Investor-State Dispute Settlement: Addressing The Asymmetry Of ISDS, available at https://documentcloud.adobe.com/link/track?uri=urn%3Aaaid%3Ascds%3AUS%3Af165cc95-6957-4e12-a042-9ec433877725e.

Andrea Saldarriaga and Andrea Shemberg, The Urgent Need To Rethink Investment Policymaking, LSE HUMAN RIGHTS BLOG, available at https://blogs.lse.ac.uk/investment-and-human-rights/portfolio-items/the-urgent-need-to-rethink-investment-policymaking/ (Apr. 16, 2018).

Claes Cronstedt, Jan Eijsbouts, Adrienne Margolis, Martijn Scheltema, Robert C. Thompson & Steven Ratner, International Arbitration of Business and Human Rights: A Step Forward, KLUWER ARBITRATION BLOG, available at http://arbitrationblog.kluwerarbitration.com/2017/11/16/international-arbitration-business-human-rights-step-forward/ (Nov. 16, 2017).

Crina Baltag, Human Rights and Environmental Disputes in International Arbitration, KLUWER ARBITRATION BLOG, available at http://arbitrationblog.kluwerarbitration.com/2018/07/24/human-rights-and-environmental-disputes-in-international-arbitration/ (July 24, 2018).

Eric de Brabandere (Leiden University), Human Rights Counterclaims in Investment Treaty Arbitration, OXFORD INVESTMENT ARBITRATION BLOG, available at https://oxia.ouplaw.com/page/human-rights-counterclaims/human-rights-counterclaims-in-investment-treaty-arbitration (Oct. 25, 2018).

Human Rights in ISDS: Where Are We Now?, GLOBAL ARBITRATION REVIEW, available at https://globalarbitrationreview.com/article/1194453/human-rights-in-isds-where-are-we-now (July 3, 2019).

ISDS Reforms Shove Human Rights Under Corporate Red Carpet, PUBLIC SERVICES INTERNATIONAL, available at http://www.world-psi.org/en/isds-reforms-shove-human-rights-under-corporate-red-carpet (Sept 11, 2018).

Kathryn Gordon, Joachim Pohl & Marie Bouchard, Investors rights and human rights – interactions under investment treaty law, LSE HUMAN RIGHTS BLOG, available at https://blogs.lse.ac.uk/investment-and-human-rights/portfolio-items/investors-rights-and-human-rights-interactions-under-investment-treaty-law-by-kathryn-gordon-joachim-pohl-and-marie-bouchard/?portfolioID=4601 (Sept. 22, 2014).

Lacey Yong, GAR Live Lookback: Human Rights And Environmental Obligations, GLOBAL ARBITRATION REVIEW, available at https://globalarbitrationreview.com/article/1035109/gar-live-lookback-human-rights-and-environmental-obligations (Feb. 17, 2016).

Lorenzo Cotula, Rethinking investment treaties to advance human rights, available at http://isds.bilaterals.org/?rethinking-investment-treaties-to (Sept 2016).

Martin Doe, Steven Ratner & Katerina Yiannibas, Arbitrating Business and Human Rights Disputes: Public Consultation on the Draft Hague Rules on Business and Human Rights Arbitration, KLUWER ARBITRATION BLOG, available at http://arbitrationblog.kluwerarbitration.com/2019/06/27/arbitrating-business-and-human-rights-disputes-public-consultation-on-the-draft-hague-rules-on-business-and-human-rights-arbitration/ (June 27, 2019).

Naomi Briercliffe & Olga Owczarek, Human-rights-based Claims by States and "New-Generation" International Investment Agreements, KLUWER ARBITRATION BLOG, available at http://arbitrationblog.kluwerarbitration.com/2018/08/01/human-rights-based-claims-by-states-and-new-generation-international-investment-agreements/ (Aug 1, 2018).

Nicole Peart & Nastasja Suhadolnik, Closing The Gap Between Human Rights And Investment Protection: What Role For Human Rights Impact Assessments?,

Thomson Reuters, available at http://arbitrationblog.practicallaw.com/closing-the-gap-between-human-rights-and-investment-protection-what-role-for-human-rights-impact-assessments/ (May 26, 2017).

Todd Weiler, Balancing Human Rights And Investor Protection: A New Approach For A Different Legal Order, Boston College, available at https://www.bc.edu/content/dam/files/schools/law/lawreviews/journals/bciclr/27_2/08_TXT.htm.

UN experts say ISDS undermines human rights as governments meet to review it, Australian Fair Trade and Investment Network Ltd, available at https://aftinet.org.au/cms/node/1710 (Apr. 4 2019).

Country Specific Press Articles

Diana A. Desierto, A Model for Business and Human Rights through International Arbitration under the Bangladesh Accord: The 2017 Decision on Admissibility Objection in Industrial Global Union and Uni Global Union, Kluwer Arbitration Blog, available at http://arbitrationblog.kluwerarbitration.com/2017/11/28/model-business-human-rights-international-arbitration-bangladesh-accord-2017-decision-admissibility-objection-industrial-global-union-uni-global-union/ (Nov 28, 2017).

Josh Scheinert, Opinion: India Tries, And Fails, To Strengthen Sovereignty And Human Rights In International Investment Law, LSE Human Rights Blog, available at https://blogs.lse.ac.uk/investment-and-human-rights/portfolio-items/7150/?portfolioID=4601 (Feb 5, 2016).

Kabir A.N. Duggal & Laurens H. van de Ven, With Rights Come Responsibilities: Sustainable Development and Gender Empowerment under the 2019 Netherlands Model BIT, Kluwer Arbitration Blog, available at http://arbitrationblog.kluwerarbitration.com/2019/06/15/with-rights-come-responsibilities-sustainable-development-and-gender-empowerment-under-the-2019-netherlands-model-bit/ (June 15, 2019).

Turkmenistan faces BIT claim after human rights ruling, Global Arbitration Review, available at https://globalarbitrationreview.com/article/1032280/turkmenistan-faces-bit-claim-after-human-rights-ruling (Apr. 24, 2013).

www.ingramcontent.com/pod-product-compliance
Lightning Source LLC
Chambersburg PA
CBHW031331230926
51848CB00001B/187